MICROCAP MAGIC

Why the biggest returns
are in the stocks
you've never heard of

Stephen Kann

Microcap Magic

Why the biggest returns are in
the stocks you've never heard of
by Stephen Kann

Published by:
Powerhouse Publishing
5524-B Hempstead Way
Springfield, VA 22151

orders@powerhousepublishing.net
http://www.powerhousepublishing.net
703-982-0984

Unattributed quotations by Stephen Kann

ISBN Paperback Edition 978-0-9759400-6-8
ISBN Kindle Edition 978-0-9759400-4-4

First paperback printing December 2015
Printed in the United States of America

Kann, Stephen
Microcap magic, why the biggest returns are in the stocks you've never heard of
1st paperback ed.

ISBN 978-0-9759400-6-8

Cover photo: Bigstock Photo, USA. Used by permission.

Arnie,

May all your investments be winners.

Steve

Steve Kann has another winner! Microcap Magic is an informative and well-written guide to the microcap stock market. Kann explains how big money can be made in "small stocks." A worthy addition to any investor's bookshelf.

John E. Fendrich
Managing Director
Meyers Associates L.P.

Having witnessed Steve's picks first hand and watched his thought process, anyone considering investing in microcap stocks needs to read this book.

Christopher Versace
Editor, The Growth & Dividend Report
Portfolio Manager, The Thematic Growth Portfolio

[Steve showed] endless energy and took the time to dig into our background and to understand and believe.... It took a special set of eyes to see... the stock that was 10c per share and went to $13, making the company one of the most successful in the country.

Mike Blumenfeld
CEO of Sport Supply Group and other microcap public companies

FOREWORD

For more than 20 years, in one form or another, I have been actively involved in hunting down investment ideas and putting them through their paces to determine if the underlying businesses and their opportunities made sense and what share price for each offered sufficient upside to warrant getting involved in the stock. My early years were spent cutting my teeth in the institutional equity research departments of Salomon Brothers and Donaldson, Lufkin & Jenrette. Those learnings and experience followed me to Friedman, Billings, Ramsey & Co. ("FBR").

After my time at FBR came to a close, through a mutual friend I eventually met Steve Kann, and we quickly started talking about stocks. It's hard not to when you love breaking down companies and business models the way Steve does.

Yet, when he started to tell me about all these "microcap" stocks, I had to push back and say something like "Steve, no one in the institutional investment community is even looking at these things. Most investors can't buy stocks below a $5 share price and that floor is moving higher."

"That's exactly why there's so much upside there," Steve said. That's when he started to explain in masterful detail the opportunity to be had by investing in the right microcap stock, the one with a solid business model, fundamentals and strong prospects for growth over the coming 12, 24, 36 months.

Even though I understood what he was saying – savvy investors recognize they are not buying a piece of paper when you buy stock, but rather you are investing in the company behind that piece of paper – it took me a while to wrap my head around the opportunity in well-positioned microcap stocks.

After talking with and, more importantly, listening to Steve, I realized the opportunity to be had by fishing in these waters. The same rigorous work that goes into understanding businesses and how to value their shares still applied, but it opened a vast new array of companies to me that were underfollowed by the institutional investment community.

While some might say that's a bad thing, given the shift to cookie cutter and press release cut & paste "research" that is put out today, underfollowed in my mind can spell opportunity… provided you do you homework. In this case that means paying attention to what Steve has to say over the coming pages. I can tell you from experience that when it comes to investing in microcap stocks, Steve knows what he's doing and talking about.

In fact, thanks to him I had some nice profits in several microcap stocks in recent years, including RBI and USA Technologies. I simply would not have known about RBI or recognized the opportunities in them if I hadn't met and listened to Steve.

And plenty of other people have benefited from Steve's insights and work too. Eventually I asked Steve to join my independent research firm. Steve's picks during his tenure with me produced an average total return of 174.6%, which, needless to say made believers out of everyone who read his words and, more importantly, heeded his advice.

He's literally "the man who wrote the book on microcap investing." And now you've got this book in your hands. I think you'll find it to be one of the best investments of time and money you've ever made.

Christopher Versace
Editor, The Growth & Dividend Report
Portfolio Manager, The Thematic Growth Portfolio

TABLE OF CONTENTS

CASE STUDIES

PREFACE

In my first job as an eager young stockbroker I received a great deal of training, but not about stocks or the companies they represented.

No, I was taught how to sell stocks - primarily stocks that had been "vetted" by our "research department." And I learned these lessons very quickly, becoming Rookie of the Year.

A few months in, I was fortunate to be referred to a big time investor I'll call Mike. Mike was from Europe and intrigued me with exotic tales of the places I'd only read about in history books and intoxicated me with talk of the uber-rich Europeans whose millions he was responsible for investing in the United States. I saw dollar signs.

On my first "pitch call" to Mike, I had barely mentioned the name of the company when he said "I'll send you $25,000."

The next month I had another stock story to share with him. Before he let me tell him the new story, he insisted we talk about the previous stock he had bought, asking pointed questions as to why the price had slid. Many of these questions were on topics I knew little or nothing about. This went on for close to an hour as I scribbled notes madly on the back of a transaction order form.

At the end of the call, he said simply "pick me up $25,000 of whatever you're selling today."

I placed the order and then spent the rest of the day annoying the management team and research department with those same pointed questions. Mike invested another $50,000 over the next couple of months, each time spending an hour or more on the phone with me. I was starting to feel more like his pet project than his stockbroker.

Mike lost more than half of the money invested in those first few stocks. It took about six months for that result to manifest itself, and the longer it went on the harder it was for me to call him, to face him. Then one day he called me and suggested we meet for breakfast. I was terrified. Was this connected European zillionaire going to have me whacked in the parking lot on the way in to the diner for losing his money? It turned out that I needn't have been afraid. Something truly astonishing happened.

When I sat down to breakfast and started yammering and trying to apologize to Mike, he stopped me and asked, "Have the questions I've put to you helped you to learn? Has the money I've lost taught you anything about how things work with these stocks?"

I told him it had and summarized what I thought I had learned. He said, "Good, consider then that I have paid your tuition for this education. Now go make me money." And make money we did, an awful lot of it.

Mike had spurred me with those questions on that first stock, questions I had never known before to ask. And I haven't stopped asking since.

The strategies you'll read about in this book have allowed me to have one of the best stock picking records in the industry. My average published stock pick has generated annualized returns of more than 80%. Even if an investor had bought everyone one of my picks and held them until the date of this writing, without acting on my sell recommendations, the returns are 57% per year.

How I went from hack salesman to prodigious stock picker is laid out in the pages that follow. The information and expertise I've gleaned from 25 years of asking questions, refining the answers and living with the results both - good and bad - dear reader, are my investment in you.

Your tuition is paid. Now go make yourself some money.

Steve Kann

INTRODUCTION

In 1987 I was a previously successful, yet out-of-work, 23-year old salesperson. Having grown bored during a stint selling corporate season tickets (what we affectionately referred to as "perforated cardboard") for the Washington Bullets (now Wizards) of the National Basketball Association, I was now looking to make "real money." Looking around at my options for a sales career – computers, printers, phone service, cars, advertising – left me pretty uninspired.

Sensing my frustration, my girlfriend at the time, later to become my wife and then my ex-wife, suggested that I look into becoming a stockbroker, because a sorority sister of hers had two brothers who were each making six figures, good money today and absolutely great money by 1987 standards ($22,000 was a typical starting salary for newly minted college graduates back then).

At first, this seemed like an unlikely path; I had a writing degree, not a business or finance degree. However, upon further reflection and having been reminded by my friends and family, I realized that I had been quite a business-minded young man, having had the cliché paper route, a lawn mowing business, a music venture and an unceremonious introduction to the world of door-to-door sales – selling jewelry (yes, really). I had even formed a marketing company with a Bullets/Wizards compatriot to sell an eyeglass/sunglass widget called the "Eyeglass Caddy" before compartments for glasses were built into virtually every car on the road.

As a good friend said at the time, "you like sales and you like business, so why don't you sell businesses, which is essentially what stockbrokers do?" (I discovered later that this is all most stockbrokers do – sell - doing very little of their own analysis, responsibility for which is ceded to the bean counter, analyst types in the best of cases and to no one at all in the worst of cases).

So, I interviewed with three different stock brokerage firms, two of which were "wire houses" (household names) and one of which was an "OTC firm" (never heard of them). All three offered me a position – this was, after all, during the great "Reagan bull market" of the 1980s, and most investment firms were hungry for new sales blood, fodder for the capitalist machine. I chose the OTC firm, which specialized in raising capital through small IPOs (initial public offerings) for "emerging growth companies," which I soon found out meant speculative, you-can-lose-all-your-money companies but which held legitimate promise.

After several weeks of training and studying, I found myself a licensed securities professional – cold calling from the floor (the chairs and desks were delivered three days late but the phones were hooked up!) through a local chamber of commerce directory - about 15 minutes (okay, six months) before the Black Monday crash of October 1987, which saw the Dow Jones Industrial Average shed 22.6% of its value in a single day, the largest one-day percentage drop in Wall Street history. Welcome to the world of high finance, young man.

A funny thing happened that day and that week, though. As we rookies were hiding under our desks afraid to talk to clients, my firm and its banking and sales leadership soldiered on through an IPO (Initial Public Offering) it had committed to underwrite (Holiday RV Superstores, NASDAQ: RVEE), promulgating the firm's philosophy that a high quality individual company that grows over time will drive appreciation into its stock price regardless of what happens in the broader market, especially in the short term.

Inexplicably to me at that time, the $6 million IPO was not just completed but oversold, meaning there was more demand for the newly issued shares than there were shares available to be sold, and the stock closed at a 40% premium to its offering price just one week after the crash. The lesson I learned from the experience, and I was fortunate to learn it early in my career, is that an individual stock is not "the market." If you buy a quality, growing company's stock at an attractive price relative to its inherent value and growth rate, you're likely to make a profit eventually, regardless of how the broader market performs.

So, here's Fundamental #1 in my methodology: I buy stocks; I do not buy the market.

Not to put too fine a point on it, if you buy Company X's stock at $1, and Company X grows to be five times larger in revenue and earnings in three years, your investment is likely to soar even if "the market" declines. A weak market might dampen the return, but, directionally, you'll be far ahead of "the market."

One caveat: the larger the company, the more its stock will behave like or "track" the market, because its fortunes are much more closely tied to macroeconomic factors – what's going on in the larger economy. For instance, if the economy is in recession, General Motors will basically track the market, because it's so big that essentially it is the market – or at least a proxy for the market. You can only "beat the market" if you buy shares in companies that are growing faster than the market (and/or stocks priced at a substantial discount to comparable companies – more on this later), and smaller companies – small caps and microcaps – are much better able to grow rapidly than companies that are already mature in their industries/geographic markets.

MICROCAP VS. MAINSTREAM

Stock Market Background

Since 1926, "small cap" stocks have outperformed their "large cap" counterparts by a wide margin. In any 15-year holding period, small stocks have outperformed large stocks in absolute and inflation-adjusted terms, whether measured by a "buy once" and hold strategy or by a "period purchase" (the same dollar amount every year).

TABLE 1. SMALL VS. LARGE: AFTER-INFLATION GROWTH OF $1 (1926-1996)

		Small Stocks: Real Growth of $1			Large Stocks: Real Growth of $1			% of Times
Holding Period (Yrs)	No. of Periods	Hold. Period Average ($)	Hold. Period Minimum ($)	% of Times < Inflation (%)	Hold. Period Average ($)	Hold. Period Minimum ($)	% of Times < Inflation (%)	Small Beat Large (%)
1	71	1.14	0.41	29.6	1.09	0.63	32.4	56.3
5	67	1.84	0.26	17.9	1.47	0.61	20.9	58.2
10	62	2.96	0.68	9.7	2.19	0.68	11.3	66.1
15	57	5.19	0.94	3.5	3.20	0.92	7.0	78.9
20	52	8.62	2.17	0.0	4.50	1.18	0.0	94.2
25	47	14.11	3.36	0.0	6.26	1.98	0.0	97.9
30	42	24.36	5.88	0.0	8.73	3.59	0.0	95.2
35	37	39.85	13.44	0.0	11.79	5.59	0.0	100.0
40	32	60.63	23.80	0.0	15.94	9.20	0.0	100.0

TABLE 2. SMALL VS. LARGE: AFTER-INFLATION GROWTH OF $1 INVESTED ANNUALLY (1926-1996)

		Small Stocks: Real Growth of $1 Annual Inv			Large Stocks: Real Growth of $1 Annual Inv			% of Times
Holding Period (Yrs)	No. of Periods	Hold. Period Average ($)	Hold. Period Minimum ($)	% of Times < Inflation (%)	Hold. Period Average ($)	Hold. Period Minimum ($)	% of Times < Inflation (%)	Small Beat Large (%)
1	71	1.14	0.41	29.6	1.09	0.63	32.4	56.3
5	67	7.48	1.66	17.9	6.34	3.06	19.4	58.2
10	62	20.24	5.28	4.8	15.92	6.21	11.3	67.7
15	57	42.01	11.31	1.8	29.96	10.94	10.5	70.2
20	52	79.08	21.95	0.0	51.01	18.64	5.8	92.3
25	47	136.47	42.57	0.0	80.86	28.45	0.0	100.0
30	42	238.28	71.35	0.0	120.40	46.17	0.0	100.0
35	37	395.86	167.30	0.0	165.63	84.19	0.0	100.0
40	32	652.18	268.27	0.0	218.53	135.83	0.0	100.0

Source: American Association of Individual Investors

In many shorter hold periods, small stocks have similarly outperformed large ones, including the five years ended at the time of this writing.

Index Name	5 Years (As of September 27, 2012)
Russell 2000 Index	10.44%
Russell Microcap Index	12.18%
S&P 500	-5.74%

Source: Google Finance

The Russell 2000 Index measures the performance of approximately 2,000 small-cap companies in the Russell 3000 Index, which itself is made up of 3,000 of the biggest U.S. stocks. The Russell 2000 is often cited as a benchmark for small-cap stocks in the United States. The weighted average market cap (market capitalization - the total dollar value of all shares held by all shareholders, internal and external, of a company) for companies in the Russell 2000 is about $1.3 billion.

The Russell Microcap Index measures the performance of the smallest 1,000 companies in the Russell 2000, plus 1,000 smaller U.S.-based listed stocks. The weighted average market capitalization for companies in the Russell Microcap is about $268 million.

The Standard & Poors 500 Index ("S&P 500") measures the performance of a select group of stocks of some of the largest companies in the United States (and the world for that matter) and is what many people consider to be the definition of "the market."

What is a microcap stock?

Some people mistake microcap stocks for "penny" stocks. While almost all penny stocks are microcap stocks, not all microcap stocks are penny stocks. By strict definition a microcap stock is defined by its market capitalization; that is, the number of shares outstanding multiplied times the stock's current quoted price. The "cap" in microcap is short for "capitalization" and the "micro" means "very small." Everyone seems to have his/her own definition of "micro" in the context of market capitalization. Here is how I, personally, see it:

Large cap – >$10 billion

Mid cap – $1.5 – $10 billion

Small Cap – $300 million – $1.5 billion

Microcap – $50 – $300 million

Nanocap – <$50 million

For purposes of this book, I'm including nanocaps in the microcap discussion, as most of the strategies, opportunities – and pitfalls – are the same. A common definition of "penny stocks" is stocks priced at $1 or less. So a $1.00 stock with 100 million shares outstanding ($100 million market cap) is both a penny stock and a microcap. However, a $6 stock with 10 million shares outstanding ($60 million market cap) is a microcap but is not a penny stock. In October 2009, Sirius XM Satellite Radio (NASDAQ: SIRI) was a penny stock ($0.58) but by no means a microcap ($2.2 billion market cap) – as of May 15, 2014 it is trading at $3.00/$19 billion.

My strongest suggestion, then, is to focus on market cap, for this is the true price of the company – the price you would have to pay to buy all of its shares (we'll set aside company debt for the moment). The share price merely represents how many units that true price is divided into.

Why should I learn about microcap stocks?

There are more than 14,000 stocks traded on the various exchanges/quotation systems in the United States (Source: Bloomberg). Only 30 stocks make up the Dow Jones Industrial Average, 500 the S&P 500 and 2,000 the Russell 2000 Index. A total of about 4,400 have "senior listings" (NYSE, AMEX, NASDAQ).

This leaves almost 10,000 stocks that trade "over the counter" (OTCQB, OTCQX, Pink Sheets), most of them microcaps, meaning that to exclude microcaps is to exclude two thirds of the investable universe in the United States. Admittedly, many microcaps are highly speculative, but there are also many that are unique, well-run companies, which are experiencing growth rates and profitability often far in excess of their larger peers but which happen to be obscure or underfollowed.

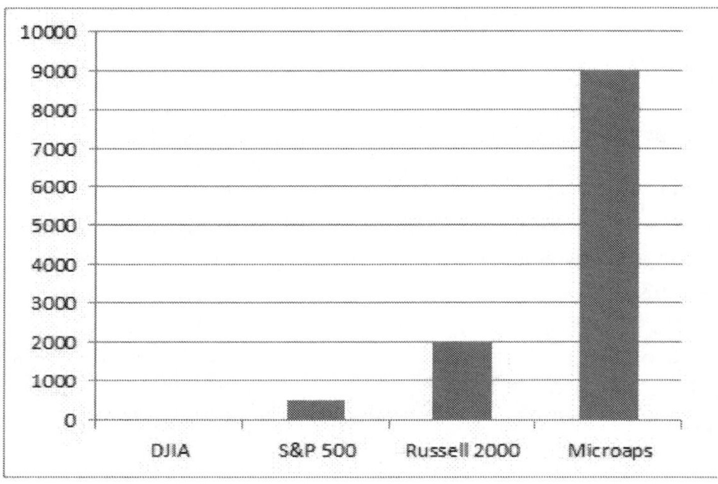

Further to the point, of the several thousand microcaps traded in the United States, it is estimated that fewer than 20% of them – less than 1,000 – have even a single independent (not paid for - more on this later) sell-side analyst "covering" the stock; that is, providing commentary and/or analysis on the company and recommendations regarding the value of, and/or trading strategies for, the stock.

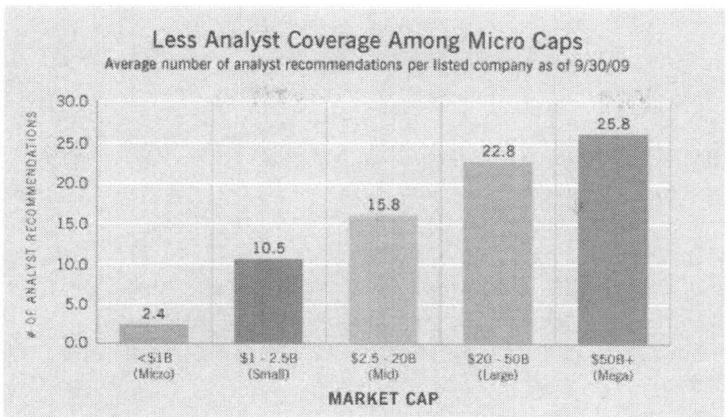

Source: Bloomberg

Which leads me to one of the most important characteristics of, and opportunities in, microcap stocks.

Information Arbitrage

Central to my thesis as to why there are significant, market-outperforming results to be gained from investing in microcaps is the idea of information arbitrage. Arbitrage, broadly defined, is profit-making by buying a security at a low price in one market and simultaneously selling the security in another market at a higher price. While I'm taking a bit of literary license here to make a point, information arbitrage with respect to investing in microcaps is defined as profit-making by buying a security at a low price in one market, when information/insight on that security is scarce and/or narrowly distributed and later selling that security at a higher price in the same market when information/insight on that security is plentiful and/or widely distributed.

Please note that this most emphatically does not mean "inside information" (information not available to the investing public) but rather information that is readily available to those who look for it, information on companies about which very few people are even aware, let alone companies that most investors take the time and effort necessary to properly research and evaluate.

Example:

You're in a one-stop-light town in Kansas and come across an "earthy" citizen named Gus at a gas station there who has an ounce of gold he got from his grandfather years ago. Gus has no TV, no radio, no Internet and doesn't read the paper. He's shocked when you offer him $300 for that little ounce of gold because the service manager standing next to Gus, who is also thin on facts, laughs and says he wouldn't give $10 for it. You buy the gold for $300, and Gus is happy to have it. Two days later when you're back in Los Angeles, you go to the bank and sell it for $1,500.

Two key points: 1) You have to know that what is being offered is gold, and 2) you have to know that gold is worth $1,500 an ounce in an "efficient" market – a market where the sheer number of people and available information creates a consensus "market price" – like Los Angeles in our example. The fact that someone with limited information and no competing bidders is willing to sell you gold at $300 an ounce, and none of the limited other parties in this "inefficient market" realize its value does not change the fact that its inherent, or "market," value is there.

Imagine if the same conversation with the man had happened at the bank branch in town and the people who overheard the conversation were the bank president, a goldsmith and a commodities trader passing through town. Would you have been able to buy the gold for $300? Would there have been any information arbitrage to exploit? Of course not – the gold would have been bid up to a price closer to its inherent or market value. Where there is plentiful information in the hands of a sufficiently large pool of people with appropriate specialized knowledge, markets are close to being efficient. A tiny country gas station with one uneducated bystander does not make for an efficient market. The microcap stock universe is not an efficient market for what you'll see are rather similar reasons.

Think of it – there are 30 analysts covering Dell, Inc. (NASDAQ: DELL). Not a single analyst covers Calpian, Inc. (OTCQB: CLPI), a company in the global payments space, which owns the largest, fastest growing mobile payments platform in India, in fact, the world (Disclaimer: CLPI is my largest personal holding as of this writing). In which stock are you likely to discover something that few people know? Or piece together a trend that hasn't been spotted by ten other analysts and distributed to thousands of institutional investors worldwide? This is what gives rise to what I refer to as information arbitrage and is my basis for investing in microcap stocks.

Case Study: Dialysis Corporation of America (NASDAQ: DCAI)

In 2003, when I was Editor (and the only writer) for Bull Market Microcap Review, I discovered DCAI through a stock screen I regularly run to find opportunities that meet at least the starting criteria for a stock I'll cover (more on this screening process later). DCAI was a high-growth company growing earnings at 50% per year, but, following some of my key valuation metrics (also to be discussed later), the stock performance was lagging far behind the company's growth on a relative basis.

Not only were the internal factors (actual company performance, growth, price) pointing to an undervalued stock, but the external factors (the growth of the overall market the company operated in and favorable, changing demographics) were screaming to me that the stock was worth $6 or more at that very moment based on fundamentals. However, at the time I made my recommendation, DCAI was trading at $2.95 per share and trading just a few thousand shares a day – a very illiquid stock by any measure. It was illiquid because no one knew about it - about the fundamental value proposition and relative pricing of the stock – not because the company's performance didn't warrant a higher price.

The theory of information arbitrage says that the closer information about a stock gets to being "perfectly and efficiently distributed" – that is, widely available and known to a sufficiently large base of investors interested in such stocks - the closer the stock will trade to its inherent value – like the golden nugget in our country gas station example, above.

To this point, less than 18 months after I recommended DCAI to my newsletter readers, the company came to the attention of a would-be buyer (a larger public company). It didn't take very long for word to get out to a much broader base of investors (the "crowd") that this was a great, undervalued stock. The stock I recommended in October 2003 when it was trading fewer than five thousand shares per day under $3.00 began trading three million shares per day at $25 per share by March 2005 (from just $6.00 a month earlier), reaching an intraday high of $35 or more than 1000% higher than my original recommend price.

Even way back in my stockbroker days I would hear investors say "I'll buy some when there's more volume;" however, "more volume" often defines a story that is past its peak buying opportunity. I want to be accumulating shares in quality companies when the shares are fundamentally undervalued – mispriced, regardless of volume - and be selling into other people's volume (buying) whenever it comes. To me, high volume = an efficient market (everyone knows the story). Profits, especially outsized profits, come from inefficient markets.

Summary:

Buy value when no one else is, before the crowd, and sell to the crowd at substantially higher prices. Sometimes the crowd comes in a month, sometimes in a year, sometimes in decade, and, yes, sometimes the crowd never comes, and you get stuck in a "sideways" or even failed stock. The trick is to have a position in a quality stock at a cheap price before the crowd comes in.

The challenge is that no one rings a bell right before this happens, so you have to be patient and trust your original analysis and stay with a stock you've bought until 1) the crowd comes in, driving volume and price higher or 2) the fundamentals of the company change to the point where the relative value of the shares are no longer what they were when you bought the shares. Only then, based on the story - not the stock price - changing substantially for the worse, should you become a seller.

Natural Leverage

Normally, when we hear the word leverage, we think in terms of borrowing, of debt. This is just one form of leverage – financial leverage. The best definition of leverage I've found is the following:

"The ability to influence a system, or an environment, in a way that multiplies the outcome . . . without a corresponding increase in the consumption of resources. In other words, leverage is the advantageous condition of having a relatively small amount of cost yield a relatively high level of return."

Ancient man controlled very large stones with relatively small levers, the small movement of which produced large lifting power focused on the stone.

When we think about financial leverage, small amounts of equity are used to control a large amount of an asset, with debt being placed as a lever to exert a large lifting power on the investment returns on the equity being risked to purchase the asset.

While financial leverage often can be utilized judiciously to boost return on equity, there are a two specific challenges with it: 1) just as a small uptick in the value of a leveraged asset can produce large returns on equity, so too will a small downtick in the value of a leveraged asset can wipe out all equity 2) one must have the creditworthiness and repayment capacity to borrow a sufficient amount of money to take advantage of leverage in the purchase of an asset, which is often outside the reach – and usually beyond the good sense - of individual investors.

What I prefer is "natural leverage." This is leverage inherent in certain investments, and to the point of this book, in certain microcap stocks. With $1,000, can you buy more shares of a $1 stock or a $10 stock?

No, that's not an IQ test. The idea of leverage is to control more of an asset with the equity capital you have available to put to work. So if I can control 1,000 shares of a high-growth, quality $1 stock vs. 100 shares of a high growth, quality $10 stock, I'm going to earn a lot more on my equity for every $0.10 move in the share price.

Also, if we assume that these two stocks are capitalized in the same way (the same number of shares outstanding), and are trading at comparable relative valuations (multiple of revenue, let's say, with the $1 company generating $10 million and the $10 company generating $100 million revenue), all other things being equal (product quality, market size, competitive landscape, profit margins), which company more easily doubles in size? Let's say that at "maturity" – even if our $1 company takes a few years longer to get there - both companies generate $1 billion in revenue and have their shares trading at $100. My 1,000-share block of the $1 stock has produced a 10,000% return, while my 100-share block of the $10 stock has produced 1000%. That is natural leverage – controlling large blocks of stock in quality companies and doing so early, before the crowd.

In 1982, shares in MCI Corporation traded at $0.25/share, while AT&T traded around $60/share (split adjusted). Within a decade both MCI and AT&T shares traded at hundreds of dollars per share (split adjusted). However, $10,000 investors in MCI owned 40,000 shares, while AT&T investors owned 1,600 shares with the same $10,000 original investment. This is natural leverage.

This is why I chuckle (to myself) when I hear people say they've bought one share of Berkshire Hathaway (NYSE: BER-A) for $125,000 dollars. Berkshire is a fine company, but it already has $150 billion in revenue; what are the odds that the company, and therefore its share price, will double or triple in any reasonable period of time? And when and if it does, you own … exactly … one share. That's not leverage.

HOW TO FIND MICROCAP WINNERS

Microcap Analysis

I have a simple and straightforward process I use, but yours should vary based on your own areas of expertise, investment horizon and objectives, as well as risk tolerance.

Check in with your financial advisor, but remember he/she is often primarily a salesperson selling someone else's money management services.

Here's how I do it:

- Initial Screen – $25-250 million market cap, price, >20% revenue growth, >$0 Earnings Before Interest, Tax, Depreciation, Amortization (EBITDA), <1.0 P/S (price-to-sales), <1.0 PE/G, limited (<30% current institutional ownership)

- Narrow the Field – exclude esoteric industries or industries I don't understand (biotech, hardcore tech like semiconductor fabrication, oil and gas).

- Zero In – overlay macro industry/sector information – I like any company growing revenue faster than its sector (providing that gross profit margins are maintained and revenue increases outpace increases in G&A expenses), some companies still growing in a declining sector, and contrarian plays such as otherwise strong companies in industries that have been beaten up but are due to cycle upward, like consumer retail in the mid 2000s and oil and gas in the late 80s.

- Secondary Screen – further due diligence including review of financial statements, "comparables" (companies in the same basic industry), major shareholders, web site, product reviews, management bios.

- Tertiary Screen – Review of SEC filings to identify land mines (more on this, below).

- Ideally, you will want to speak to management (at least the investor relations officer) to get clarification on any points and to measure overall confidence and enthusiasm for the company.

- You should care little about what the overall economy is doing and care little about what the broader stock market is doing; you're in this for the medium to long-term anyway.

- You should invest in individual companies at attractive prices relative to their growth; don't invest in the "stock market." The stock market is merely a conduit for monetizing your investment.

The PE/G Ratio

First, a word on the PE ratio (or just "PE") of a stock, or its Price-to-Earnings ratio. When we refer to earnings in this context we're talking about earnings per share ("EPS"), which is simply a company's total net income (revenue minus cost of goods minus operating expenses minus interest paid on debt minus taxes minus depreciation/amortization) divided by the number of shares outstanding (number of shares held by all shareholders, whether insiders or the public at large).

So, a company which has net income of $10 million and 10 million shares outstanding has $1.00 in earnings per share. If the earnings were simply distributed to shareholders, everyone would get $1.00 per share. The PE ratio is a company metric for figuring at a glance the relative pricing of a share of stock.

Stocks with low PEs are often said to be "cheap" and stocks with high PEs are often said to be "expensive." However, the PE tells only part of the story, for not all earnings per share are created equally when viewed through the lens of the relative current and future value of a stock.

This is where the PE/G ratio comes in. Simply described, the PE/G ratio is the relationship of a stock's price-to-earnings ratio to growth and is one of my absolutely favorite metrics to find microcap winners. The premise is this: a low price to earnings ratio – a common but, in my opinion, misused metric – in a vacuum is irrelevant, and has meaning only when evaluated in the context of the growth of the company. This is because a fast growing company's earnings have more current value than a slower growing one, because, when you buy a stock, you're buying into the company's future, not its past.

A company might generate $0.50/share in earnings today, and if it has been consistently growing at 30% per year, next year's earnings per share should be $0.65, $0.85 the year after. Therefore, today's 20 PE is misleading, because, at today's price of $10.00 ($0.50 EPS multiplied by its 20 PE), next year's PE will be just 15 (today's $10.00 price divided by next year's $0.65 EPS) and the year after's PE will be less than 12. We call this "Forward PE."

Compare this to a company currently trading at a 15 PE (let's say $15 and EPS of $1.00). It only looks cheaper, because, after accounting for its growth of only 10%, giving next year an estimated EPS of $1.10 and the following year just $1.21, it's actually trading at a Forward PE of 14 and 12 respectively.

Therefore, these two stocks, one of which has a higher PE than the other, are priced almost identically on a relative growth basis – in both cases we're buying about the same proportion of future profits. Simply put, I'm willing to pay more for faster growth and the PE/G ratio gives me the best barometer of the price I'm actually paying for a stock.

Looking For Inflection Points

Inflection points, or moments of dramatic change, especially in the development of a company, industry or market, can provide key entry points into a stock. I will sometimes disregard historical profitability if I find a compelling inflection point. Some obvious inflection points include regulatory or patent approval of a company's product, a significant enhancement to the management team, distribution and/or product line, the settling of a potentially devastating law suit, winning a key law suit, etc.

Any one of these events could portend sudden new traction for a company's business, leading it to higher revenue and earnings and/or enhancing its appeal as an acquisition target, either of which tends to lead to higher stock prices (if you've bought the stock at an attractive price to begin with).

Less dramatic and immediate are inflection points such as a company beginning to realize meaningful operating leverage, meaning revenue growth is outpacing growth in operating costs. For instance, a company might spend years investing in its manufacturing capabilities and infrastructure to support as much as $100 million in sales, but it is currently generating only $50 million in sales. The company's investing in its future has been a drag on earnings, but now it's done spending and can grow sales dramatically without any further investment, dropping larger, higher margin and accelerating profits to the bottom line.

Or a company might have just gone through a large cost restructuring, the positive effects of which aren't obvious or unappreciated, especially in thinly traded, barely followed stocks. In many cases, much of every new dollar in sales drops directly to the bottom line – if they company's products have a gross profit margin of 40%, much of that 40% will drop directly to the bottom line because the money has already been spent in previous quarters to support the increase in sales.

MICROCAP LAND MINES

Convertible debt and/or preferred equity

Convertible securities and convertible preferred shares (stock that has different and superior rights to common shares) represent potential dilution (or reduction in relative ownership leading to a devaluation of shares) to shareholders who own common shares prior to such conversion. Conversion in this case means the exchange of a senior (collateralized) or preferred security for shares of common stock.

The potential effect of such conversion can be highly and negatively impactful to shareholders at the time. For example: If XYZ Corp. has 5,000,000 shares outstanding at $5, its market cap is $25 million. However, if XYZ Corp. also has a note outstanding in the amount of $5,000,000, which is convertible into shares at $1 per share (5 million potential new shares), such note's conversion would result in XYZ Corp. having 10,000,000 shares outstanding at the same $5, making its market cap $50 million.

Of course, the balance sheet has improved, but the company's market value has doubled (perhaps unreasonably so) while your shares have not increased in price at all and, in fact, may reduce when the market cap is "normalized" or floats back to the $25 million market value the stock had prior to the introduction of additional shares. And any earnings will now be distributed over twice as many shares, cutting EPS in half (this is what the notation "fully diluted EPS" is designed to identify in income statements – the EPS if all such convertible and other derivative securities were to be converted/exercised).

If the market sees this instant creation of new shares and its impact on earnings as now over-valuing the company, the share price can and usually will come under pressure. Much depends on the conversion price. If the conversion price is above where the current share price is, the convertible security is said to be "under water" and unlikely to convert, as there is no profit to be gained from converting. However, if the conversion price is stated as a percentage discount to the price at the time of conversion instead of a fixed price, there is likely to be severe pressure on the stock, because there is unknown and potentially unlimited dilution to existing shareholders.

Example: A convertible note holder with the right to convert into common shares at "a 30% discount at the time of such conversion" with no price specified will always book a profit upon conversion regardless of stock price. Such a convertible security with no set conversion price is also called a "death spiral," because its existence puts pressure on the stock (there's a profit-locked potential seller at all times), which further lowers the price and therefore potential conversion price, which puts further pressure on the stock, which further lowers the potential conversion price, etc.

Dilutive warrant/options

The land mine with warrants/options is similar in almost every respect to those of convertible securities, except that most warrants/options have a fixed price and time horizon.

Pending Registration Statement

A registration statement (usually Form S-1 or Form S-3) is what a company files with the SEC to make freely tradable those share which were previously unissued (shares offered in an IPO or secondary offering) or restricted from resale (shares acquired at an earlier date by private investors in the company).

Here is where your reading of SEC filings is so important: most investors who make private investments in a public company will require that the company grant said investor "piggyback" and/or "demand" registration rights. Piggyback means that if the company files any registration statement with the SEC the company must include the investors then-restricted shares in the registration statement, which allows the investor to sell any or all their shares at will after the registration statement is declared "effective" by the SEC.

Basically, "effective" means only that the information contained in the registration statement has been deemed "complete," not that the SEC has passed on the merits of the shares or offering. "Demand" registration rights means exactly what it sounds like, that the investor may demand that the company file a registration statement at any time and/or upon certain conditions.

The point is that you must review all of a company's SEC filings, particularly those pertaining to financings, in which filings you'll be able to find such potential land mines. What might these land mines affect your investment you ask? Read on.

In 2014, a public company my firm knew well went to Europe to stir up investor support for its shares and spent over $200,000 of investor capital in the effort (not uncommon among microcap stocks - more on this in the chapter "Investor Relations").

However, undisclosed to investors the company met with in Europe (or rather unknown to those investors who didn't take the time to review the company's SEC filings), the company had filed a registration statement covering almost 29 million shares! This quadrupled the number of shares in the float – the number of shares available to trade hands between public investors.

In other words, the supply of shares dramatically increased, and increased far in excess of whatever demand the company was hoping to create in going to Europe in the first place. And you know what happens when there's a large imbalance of supply and demand? Predictably the stock plummeted by half within days of the registration statement being declared effective.

You'll notice that the above "land mines" have to do with a sudden increase in the number of shares that may be sold into the market without restriction. That alone is enough to weigh on a stock price and, given the relative lack of liquidity/demand for many microcaps, weight it down potentially for a long time.

Further and more insidious to your interests is that just about any existing restricted shares that are included in a registration statement (in contrast to simply previously authorized shares that have not been yet issued to anyone) will invariably be owned by the holder of such shares at a much lower cost basis than the then-current price, creating a lot of incentive to take some amount of money off the table – even if they still love the stock.

Imagine the first private investors in the company who 1) bought the shares at, say, $0.10/share 2) have owned the shares for three years. Let's say the quoted price of the shares is $1.75. Such investors would be happy to sell their shares at just about any price above $0.20 and do so at a huge profit. In other words, they don't mind "crushing the bid" of such a stock because just about any price is an acceptable price for them to sell.

Ballooning Notes

This is debt that must be paid off in full at a specific point in time, usually a term of just a few years, not amortized down to zero over many years like a traditional mortgage or car loan you're familiar with. You can find details on the nature of a company's debt in the "Notes to Financial Statements" of quarterly and annual reports filed by the company with the SEC. If a company has a $7 million balloon note coming due on 12/31/09, it's November 15, 2009 and the company has only $1 million in cash, it might indicate that the company is about to experience a severe financial crisis.

Insider Selling

An often reliable indicator of what's going on with the fundamentals of a company is when "insiders" (officers, directors and shareholders holding more than 10% of the outstanding shares) are selling or buying shares in the company. Insiders are required to report their purchases and sales of the company's stock to the SEC on "Form 4."

Most consumer-oriented financial sites (Yahoo! Finance, Google Finance, etc.) summarize such insider activity under one of the common tabs. For instance, the company's Chief Financial Officer is regularly buying blocks of stock around the current price may well be a good sign that the company is heading in the right direction.

Of course, the converse may be true – selling blocks of stock may indicate a company in trouble. Note: that insiders are required to report purchases when they're simply exercising previously granted stock options, often a price far below current market prices; I wouldn't read much into such purchases about the strength of the company, as the insider is realizing an instant paper profit from such exercise regardless of his or her long term confidence in the company or lack thereof.

Paid-for Research

A much sought after prize for microcap public companies is getting picked up for research coverage (ongoing monitoring, reporting and analysis by one or more analysts). However, all research coverage is not created equal. I want to highlight three basic forms research and their differences.

The first is one most are familiar with, which is when a full-service broker dealer (Morgan Stanley, Merrill Lynch, etc.) publishes a research report on a company. There are potential conflicts of interest in this form, as when the company has had or later has an investment banking relationship with the broker dealer, notwithstanding SEC rules addressing the potential conflicts. However, on the whole, the information, work and analysis in this type of research are often professional and of good quality.

The second, and in my opinion most valuable, is research produced by truly independent research firms. By independent I mean that it's a firm that does nothing but research and sells its research for cash to investors; they have no investment banking, no trading and no conflicts, giving such firms the opportunity to have a truly independent voice.

The third and potentially most concerning form of research is that which is paid for by the company itself to a "for hire" research firm. Ostensibly, the research firm will "call it as it sees it," and the payment is often defined as "covering hard costs" incurred by the research firm or a "due diligence" fee, but in the end the company is paying to have research created about it.

Many "paid for" research firms actually do very good work (i.e. Taglich Brothers), but there is an inherent potential conflict of interest in such relationships in that, if the research firm writes too many negative reports about their clients, they won't have much success in attracting new clients.

Let's face it, if a company is paying to have a firm produce a research report, they want the report to represent the company in the best light possible in order to stimulate buying in the stock. Still, not all paid for "research" even pretends to be "objective." Many investor relations firms (or "financial public relations firms") simply produce puff pieces for the company, which appear to be research reports. Beware.

Fortunately, several years ago the SEC began requiring such reports to bear a disclaimer stating that the report has been paid for, so look closely for such disclaimers in very fine print somewhere in the report.

Aggressive or "Empty" Investor Relations and PR

What I mean here is a company that constantly makes press releases that are high on sizzle but low on steak. Announcements of every new "strategic alliance" or every new "entry into xyz market" or new brand development. I often half-joke about releases which trumpet that a company has "convened a panel to discuss the development of a new business line into which it is considering an entry in order to capitalize on a $1 billion market opportunity" or some other such empty nonsense.

Also be on the lookout for press releases that talk all about the market and not about the company, such as "our Gizmo product line addresses the $18 billion international home healthcare market, which, according to a recent study by the Harvard Business School, is growing at 28% annually and is expected to top $30 billion within five years" – this is misdirection.

Seeing two or three of these type of press releases over the course of a few weeks, with no substantive developments (those which translate into actually revenue for the company) usually gets me running for the hills. Related to this are any stocks recommended in a seemingly objective newsletter sent to your home that recommends a particular stock.

Look again at the fine print at the end of such newsletters and you will usually find that the newsletter publisher has been paid by the company or, more often, a third party on behalf of the company.

TRICKS OF THE TRADE

Transitional Market Caps

This is one of my favorite things to look for. What I call a transitional market cap is one that is barely below one of the widely followed triggers among institutional investors. What many individual investors don't know is that most funds have covenants – rules they've agreed to follow when raising capital for their fund.

These rules sometimes include targeted or excluded sectors (the fund "will focus on investments in consumer retail" or "will not invest in real estate or oil and gas"), geographies ("the fund will not invest in companies headquartered outside of the United States"), and even moral restrictions ("the fund will invest only in companies that have 'earth-friendly' policies, practices and products").

A rule that most funds have is related to market cap, as in the fund will not invest in any company with a market cap of less than X. "X" typically falls along predictable lines with the following "breakpoints:" $50 million, $100 million, $250 million, $500 million, $1 billion and so on. The higher up the breakpoint ladder you go, the more funds there are that are interested in at least looking at the name (the stock).

Presuming that the company is quality and undervalued, the more investors looking into and following the story by definition leads to more investors interested, which in turn leads to more investors analyzing the story, which leads to more people owning and/or trading the stock.

So I like to look for companies that I believe are undervalued and have market caps in the $40mms, the $90mms, the low $200mms, etc., the premise being that a small move higher in the stock will push it through that next "tripwire," at which point more eyes with deeper pockets will be on the stock. If I'm right about the stock being undervalued, I will often see the stock's move higher accelerated.

Transitional Prices

Similarly to transitional market caps, but to a lesser extent, there are "transitional prices," above which a different set of investors will begin to consider a stock. $1.00 per share is the price above which a stock may remain listed on NASDAQ, so be very careful about buying stocks at or near $1.00 on NASDAQ, as there is a risk that a small erosion in price would cause a "de-listing" from NASDAQ, resulting in the shares being subject to far less liquidity on a lesser market like the OTCQB, etc.

Conversely, $3.00 per share is the price above which a stock may gain an initial listing – or "up-listing" - on the NYSE MKT (formerly, the American Stock Exchange), subject to other initial listing requirements, so a stock that meets the other listing requirements and trades at, say, $2.90 might soon move up to the NYSE MKT, improving its "status" and opening the stock up to much more potential liquidity.

$5.00 per share is the price above which a security may be margined (meaning a buyer can buy twice as many shares with the same cash in his account, borrowing the rest of the cash needed from his brokerage firm) and the price above which a stock may not be considered a "penny stock" and subject to the onerous purchasing rules imposed on such transactions by FINRA and most brokerage firms. So, a stock trading at, say, $4.75 may soon be more widely available for purchase by investors and in greater share amounts.

UNDERSTANDING HOW TO EXECUTE MICROCAP TRADES

Exactly how stocks are quoted and traded on NASDAQ or Over-the-Counter (OTCQX, OTC Bulletin Board, Pink Sheets) is often quite alien to the typical individual investor. Most investors focus on the most visible price associated with a particular stock – the "last trade," which is the most recent trade and the price that typically appears directly next to a stock in most trading platforms and/or quote services. The last trade of the day is the "Closing Price," which is the price that used to be printed in newspapers the following morning. However, this is just one price associated with a stock and tells only a part of the story.

The other prices to pay attention to when actually preparing to buy a stock are the "Bid" and the "Offer" (also called the "Ask," the price current shareholders are "asking" for their shares).

A Bid is the price at which one or more investors are willing to buy stock; they're literally bidding for shares at that price from the market – existing shareholders who own the stock.

The Offer is the price investors who currently own shares of a stock are "asking" for their shares from the market – potential buyers of the stock. Hence, the Bid is always lower than the

Offer, because if an investor were to "bid" for stock at a price equal to the current Offer price, they'd simply buy the shares from the shareholder offering shares at that Offer price rather than posting a Bid looking to buy shares.

When you see the shares of XYZ quoted $3.00-$3.25, what you're looking at is the "inside quote." That is, you're looking at the highest posted Bid ($3.00) being made by a wannabe shareholder and the lowest posted Offer ($3.25) being made by a current shareholder. As a potential buyer of shares of XYZ, you'd have two options here; you can either buy the number of shares available at the Offer price or you can post – or rather have you stockbroker post – a new, higher Bid at, say, $3.10, in hopes that some current shareholder will be willing to sell you the shares you want at the new, higher Bid price.

But wait, there's more. Each Bid and Offer comes with a "Size" quoted, since not all shareholders are seeking to buy or sell the same number of shares. In the above example, XYZ shares available at the Offer price might be only 500 shares, above which number of shares there may be no additional shares available from any seller at this price. This is what causes a stock to move up or down, when shares available at a particular quoted price are bought and no more remain, leaving the next lowest Offer price as the newly quoted price in the "inside quote."

Which leads us to another point. At any given time there may be many other levels of prices of shares being Bid and Offered (see end of this chapter). We only see the highest Bid and lowest Offer when we see the typical quote, but there are usually more buyers and sellers in the weeds behinds the scenes. There may be 5,000 shares Bid at $2.95, 10,000 shares Bid at $2.90 and so on. These are potential buyers who are trying to buyer shares at a price below the current "market."

These buyers may sit there at that price waiting for 1) the market to drop due to the currently Bid 500 shares at $3.00 being sold and that Bid disappearing, leaving the $2.95 as the then-highest bid or 2) a large potential seller of XYZ – a current shareholder interested in selling more than the 500 shares available at $3.00.

This shareholder could sell 500 shares at $3.00 to the first bidder and 5,000 more to the $2.95 bidder as part of one trade. The same, of course, can happen on the Offer side, where a big buyer can literally buy all shares Offered at all prices at once. This is called "clearing the offers."

Related, let's examine what happens when you place a "Limit Order." A Limit Order is just as it sounds – you're placing a price and size limit on a stock purchase. "Buy 500 shares of XYZ at $3.10" is a Limit Order, and you're instructing your broker to buy no more than 500 shares of XYZ at a maximum price of $3.10 per share. Using the above "inside quote" of $3.00-$3.25, we see that there are no shares currently being Offered for sale at $3.10. We know this because the inside quote shows the lowest Offer.

To effect the Limit Order your broker will place an order through a "Market Maker" (either their own brokerage firm or another) which creates a new Bid for 500 shares at $3.10, and the new inside quote will moments later reflect your order as in $3.10 – $3.25. Note: if your Limit Order was for 500 shares at $2.95, your order would not affect the inside quote since your bid is lower than the highest bid currently being quoted.

So what does all this (which I realize might be rudimentary to some readers) have to do with how you should buy and sell microcap stocks?

In the above example of how the market comes up with stock quotes, we discussed only "Limit Orders." A "Market Order" is an order in which no price is specified and which is executed on behalf of a buyer or seller regardless of price. This is danger land for microcap investors because microcap stocks are often so thinly traded due to a dearth of buyers and sellers at any given time.

Real-Time Level 2 Quote Compilation

MPID	Bid Price	Size	Date/Time
MAXM	0.97	22300	11:22
CANT	0.96	1000	11:11
ETRF	0.95	2000	12:00
NITE	0.92	52500	12:12
CSTI	0.90	1000	10:21
PUMA	0.87	1000	08:10
CDEL	0.835	1000	12:35
MERI	0.82	1000	05/29
ATDF	0.01	10000	12:30
VFIN	0.0001	10000	05/15
GUGS	U		12/09

MPID	Ask Price	Size	Date/Time
ATDF	1.00	2200	12:30
CANT	1.00	100	11:11
GUGS	1.04	100	07/14
CSTI	1.08	20000	10:21
CDEL	1.23	100	12:35
NITE	1.25	9102	11:22
PUMA	1.28	100	08:10
MERI	1.75	100	03/25
MAXM	800.00	1	11:22
VFIN	2000.97	1	07/15
ETRF	U		07:50

The MPID column shows the various call signs of the market makers participating in the primary trading of this stock. This is the internal world of stock trading, often unseen by the individual investor.

MICROCAP INVESTING RULES

I thought it would be an excellent idea to discuss and emphasize some of the "dos" and "don'ts" of microcap investing – the "Rules." If you want a real chance to make above average returns on such stocks, you just have to be smart and disciplined – and have a plan.

Rule #1 – Do Diversify

Microcaps, by definition, carry higher risk. They're small companies where relatively minor issues can be highly impactful, whereas larger companies can endure the hits such as lawsuits or some negative PR issues. Small companies are less able to withstand that. So given that the risk profile is greater, it's unwise for you to buy just one or two microcap stocks, or to jump in and out of one stock and into the other (more on trying to "time" the market later).

Far and away the best strategy, I have found, is to allocate a certain fixed dollar amount to microcaps as a whole, and build a diversified portfolio of a half dozen or more well-researched, well-considered, well-priced stocks over some reasonable period of time, say, one year.

I can think back to my days as a stockbroker in the 1980s, when we typically recommended about one new microcap stock idea per month. I had a few clients, a few of which were my favorites, who literally bought only one out of every three of the recommendations, trying as they could to "divine the truth" and pick only the winners. Sure enough, a couple of clients managed to pick, with perfect precision, the dogs. Their average one-year portfolio results? About negative 30%. The average one-year portfolio results for the clients who bought all of them – every single one, winners and losers alike? About 100%.

You see, one of the stocks in the "basket" of ten went from $1 to 17 in less than a year, which would suggest – scream, actually – that the overall portfolio approach is much better than the "pick and choose" approach. This always holds true – always – so don't be the investor who gets lucky with one stock and decides you're infallible. I would consider myself a real expert in this space, and I, with all my research and all my access to management and all my experience and my highly trained eye, still don't get it right every time. In fact, it is at a virtual truism that the ones I'm sure will do the best are the ones that usually don't do the best. Conversely, the ones that I like but don't love are the ones that really outperform – where management really executes. These companies are the ones that usually become huge scores in the portfolio.

A more recent example of this was when I was running Bull Market Microcap Review, microcap investment newsletter I started for BullMarket.com. There were nine companies I initiated coverage on during my tenure there. I loved them all, but there were two in particular that were, ironically, the two largest (greatest market capitalization) companies in the portfolio.

They were both trading in the teens and trading on NASDAQ, and were sort of out of character for what I typically look for because they were larger, which supposedly meant that they were more "stable" and "less risky." Well, those were the two of three worst performing stocks out of the nine that I covered. The two I was sure that were going to do well if all else failed, did poorly;

one company saw its share price cut in half, and the other was a wipe out. Had I succumbed to gut instinct and not followed my own rule of putting equal amounts into every company regardless of how you feel about it–as long as they pass my methodology and meet my metrics – I would've been overweighted in the ones that did the worst. That would have had an overall detrimental effect on the portfolio.

The simple fact is that no one – no, not even me – knows exactly when, if, or which of the stocks will move or how much. The trick is to own the one that moves. The way to do this is to diversify and own them all.

So summarizing this "Do Diversify" rule, depending on your own risk tolerance, you should never have more than 20 percent of your portfolio's assets allocated in microcaps. Then, whatever that number is, you have to spread it around. For example, let's say you have $100,000 that is liquid and allocated to equities, and 80 percent of that is used for more conservative investments like ETFs, funds, or individual mid-cap or large cap stocks. That means no more than $20,000 in total should go into microcap stocks.

In my opinion, you want to have at least five different microcap companies to get the proper amount of diversification, but the more the better. Of course, there's the point of diminishing returns, so I'd say 20 or more microcap positions, for example, is too many. The sweet spot for diversification is between five to 10 stocks that meet the criteria outlined in this book. Do that and you'll catch your fair share of good performers, big winners, and the poor performers and wipeouts will be simply a small drag on the overall return of your portfolio, not a damaging hit to your assets.

A question that often comes up is whether it's important to diversify among industries, sectors, geography, catalysts, etc. I say that it's critical not to outsmart yourself and think you know more than the market does. Keep those allocations relatively even across whatever number of stocks you're able to buy with the money you've allocated for microcaps, and remember that discipline is the key. Since my whole methodology seeks to uncover undervalued stocks relative to current conditions, I don't think there is a need for diversification among particular drivers or among catalysts. I'm not looking only at things that drive the fundamentals of the business; what I'm really looking for right now is mispriced fundamentals.

As an example, one of the stocks I published research on when I was a contributing equity analyst for Think 20/20 was HyperCom (was NYSE:HYC, since acquired). I found the company using my filters when its shares were trading at $1.35, and when I compared it to its larger peers on a one-for-one, apples-to-apples basis, I felt that the stock at the time was worth $4 per share (as the story evolved over the following months, I subsequently raised my estimate to $6). It was ultimately acquired for $11 within 18 months.

I look for those opportunities regardless of sector and other factors, and by following that methodology, and looking for stocks that are undervalued now in terms of fundamentals, you're always going to win.

Rule #2 – Don't Let Past Picks Influence Future Ones

This rule evolved out of Rule #1 and was a lesson hard-learned (or, more probably, not learned at all) by the clients I mentioned who tried to single out winners and losers, didn't properly diversify and ultimately managed to pick the losers just about every time. They were letting the performance of the previous stock influence their decision to buy the next one. Stock A was down, so they didn't buy Stock B. Stock B doubled, so they bought Stock C. Stock C underperformed, so they didn't buy Stock D, and so on. Keep in mind two things: you buy microcap stocks that meet your criteria and then prepare yourself to hold them until they move; sometimes that may take months or even years.

One stock I discovered when I was at Bull Market Microcap Review was a company called ePlus (NASDAQ: PLUS). I loved this stock on the face of it. After I was satisfied that the company's numbers and relative price/value was attractive, I went through my normal process of researching the macro questions (the company had diversified lines in IT hardware, equipment financing, IT consulting, "eProcurement" and others, all growth areas) and then interviewing management.

In late September 2003, I published my report with the stock trading at $15, suggesting that it was worth $20 right then, and I put a 18-month price target on it of a minimum of $25. What happened? It stumbled along, for years not trading above my recommend price, even dipping into single digits. More on PLUS in a second.

To the point of this Rule, had I or a client of mine then looked at the next stock(s) that met all the criteria through the lens of PLUS' performance, we would have sat out that next one. That next one was Dialysis Corporation of America (traded NASDAQ: DCAI), which I recommended at $2.95 (split-adjusted) with a 24-month target price of $7, based on both its growth and price/value relative to its larger peers. It kept outperforming expectations operationally and my price expectation rose alongside that. DCAI was acquired at $14 per share in five years, good for a return of over 400%, or about 70% annualized. That makes up for a lot of sideways performers and the rare wipeout.

And what happened to our "loser" PLUS? It trades at almost $90 per share as of the date of this writing, nine years after I recommended it at $15. That's still good for a better than 500% return, or about 22% annually, far better than any market index over that period. And not bad for one of my "loser" picks.

The point is that making a decision on a new stock you've found through your filtering solely on the basis that the last stock that "looked like this one" hasn't moved yet is investing based on emotion, investing without discipline and is a recipe for poor returns.

Rule #3 – Don't Be a Market Timer

"Market Timing" is simply trying to divine the exact right moments to buy and sell, often jumping in and out of positions, rather than "Buy and Hold" (or "Accumulate and Hold" as I'd rather think about it), buying quality stocks at attractive prices, often accumulating shares over time, and holding them for the longer term, which in the context of buying microcaps is 2 to 5 years.

The debate about Market Timing vs. Buy and Hold is largely irrelevant to the purposes of this book in that the debate is often couched in terms of "market" performance, usually the S&P 500. However, as I've told anyone who'd listen over the years, I buy stocks not the "market."

However, since it's such a debate, it bears a mention here along with my thoughts. In my opinion, there is overwhelming evidence that timing the market is a very bad strategy for the average investor (and even for those of you who think you are above average!), as well as professional ones.

According to research conducted by Charles Schwab Company in 2012, between 1926 and 2011, a 20-year holding period never produced a negative result.

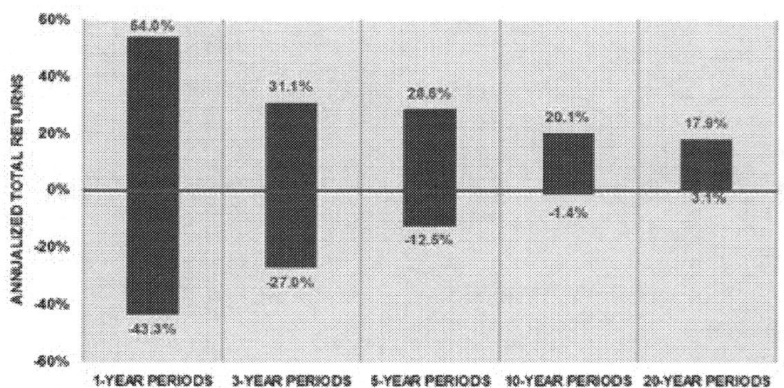

Source: Schwab Center for Financial Research

The vast majority of individual investors who try to "time" their investments are often (okay, just about always) driven by emotion and buy high – or only after a stock has moved, after it's been "validated" by the others, after it is "safe" (when the emotion is greed and the "greater fool" theory prevails) – and sell low – after they've sat paralyzed watching a stock nose dive for weeks or months (when the emotion is fear – of loss, of being proven wrong), often ignoring a negative change or changes in the fundamentals of a company, which is the only thing that matters.

This is ever truer in the microcap arena. Stocks can move so fast here. The only way to own a stock before it moves is to buy it early, usually while nobody is watching, and be prepared hang on for a while, accumulating more shares if the price relative to value warrants and personal liquidity allows.

The microcaps we are looking to buy are by definition opportunities discovered before the crowd. So we are looking to buy into fundamentals before those fundamentals are fully valued and acted upon by investors in the marketplace. The danger, if you will, of trying to market time microcaps is one of lost opportunities. Market timers want to try to buy a microcap stock the minute before it's going to move and sell it the minute it gets to its high, when the only goal should be to sell it for sufficiently more than you paid for it within a time period that generates exceptional returns. I like to remind people that nobody rings a bell when a stock is about to move or when it hits its high.

So you have to remove that greed factor from your decision-making and instead focus on the fundamentals of each particular opportunity. The mindset has to be about buying great value at a great price, before the market has fully valued the opportunity, and with the intent of being in the position when it moves to take advantage – and profits - whether that's a week, a month or even a few years later. So be prepared to hang on to the microcap stocks you buy for as long as two or three years, sometimes as long as five, in order the get the very most out of them.

Keep in mind; you are looking to buy microcaps that can generate returns of 3x, 4x, 5x, 6x or more. If you have to wait two years to get that 3x or 4x, then your annualized return is going to be outstanding. The risk with microcaps, however, is they're relatively illiquid because they are relatively (often completely) unknown. If they become known in the market – perhaps through media coverage or a major investor gets involved – then all at once, these things can move 100 percent in days or even hours. At that point, you've really lost leverage because if you are looking at a stock that is trading at $1, and it moves to $2, you've lost half your leverage. That's half as many shares as you could buy.

For me, I'd rather have bought that stock early and been content to wait until the broader market recognized the value that I already had recognized.

I can tell you several stories where patience was, literally, a golden virtue. In 1987, a stock I liked a lot, VideoSpection, Inc. (VDSP at the time, but long since acquired) was trading at $1 3/8 ($1.375 – this was before "decimalization"). I and a colleague bought up (on behalf of our clients) almost the entire float (the number of freely traded shares in the hands of the public, not officers, directors or other "control" shareholders) and the stock did nothing but fall to $0.375, where it stayed for over three long years.

In December of that third year a few investors got understandably impatient and frustrated and decided to sell the stock and just take the loss for tax purposes. And guess what happened? The company was subsumed by its subsidiary, Megahertz Corporation, in 1993 and the next year was acquired by US Robotics, which was in turn acquired by 3Com Corp. This is not an exaggeration: the stock went to $11 in 90 days (after sitting at under $0.50 for over two years!), and the company was acquired twice over the next year driving the stock up over $50/share, adjusted pro rata for share exchanges.

That's right: three years wasn't long enough, but three years and three months was, and those who held it four years (although almost no one I knew was that greedy) got about an 40x return.

Keep in mind that the story kept getting better in the years the stock was falling and going sideways, but the market hadn't recognized it yet. Similarly, the company didn't all of a sudden become 40x more valuable in mere months. The intrinsic value was always there; it just took some time for the market to catch up. If you didn't try to time it, you were in it when it exploded. Buy good stocks at good prices early and hold on to them.

So we don't know exactly when we're going to be selling to capture our profit, but when do we sell to cut our losses? The answer is simply "when the story changes." If, because of changes in the fundamentals of the company, the stock is priced higher than the underlying value as it appears relative to growth, then it's no longer an opportunity.

You have to ask yourself, as a disciplined and unemotional investor, if you're already in a stock and you wake up one day and look at it as if you were looking at it for the very first time, would you buy it today based on its fundamentals and price today if your cash wasn't locked into the stock but rather sitting in neat stacks of $100 bills on your coffee table? If the answer is, "No", and it doesn't meet your criteria, then you must sell it and use the cash, even though it's less than you invested, to invest in a company who meets your criteria today and offers you the 3x or greater return you're looking for. Every day that you choose to own a stock that you already own is exactly the same as making the affirmative decision to buy it again that day.

You can't look at a down stock as money you've lost but rather the actual amount of money you currently have to deploy, and that money is better invested in stocks that currently match what you're looking for in a microcap opportunity.

So stay focused on the fundamentals and the intrinsic value of each opportunity so that you don't get discouraged by the volatility of the stock price. Volatility means an opportunity to build a position if the story hasn't changed. You have no doubt heard of the term, "dollar-cost averaging" (the investment strategy of investing regular amounts in a stock or mutual fund at regular intervals over time) or the cruder "doubling down."

These strategies are all well and good so long as the fundamentals of the company haven't changed. People get in trouble when they throw good money after bad, and that's the discussion about the fundamentals and not about the price. The price can increase when no value has increased, and the price can decline when no value has declined. It's important to understand that and know the difference, and not be scared off by the volatility.

Keep your eye on the ball. That means focusing on the underlying growth in the company, its value relative to its peers and its price relative to its growth, and if that story hasn't changed or even has gotten better, then I would not be worried one bit about a declining price for a month, a year, or as with VDSP, even three years.

Rule #4 – Do Dollar-Cost Average Both In and Out of Positions

Part of not being a market timer is acknowledging that you will never pick the absolute bottom price a stock will trade at to buy and you'll never pick the absolute top price to sell. You simply must focus on paying a reasonable price relative to where the company is developmentally and continue to accumulate shares over time. By "developmentally," I mean to focus on how the company is actually performing, not the stock.

If the company, by virtue of its executing its business plan well and thereby driving more fundamental value into the business, a share price that doesn't move higher should be viewed as a Godsend to those who are accumulating a meaningful position. Conversely, if the company has a developmental setback (like the loss of its largest customer) you must reevaluate if the then-current stock price still reflects the underlying value of the company.

If you have $25,000 allocated to a single stock position, never buy it all at once for several reasons, not least of which is that some of these smaller stocks trade so thinly (low volume) that one single larger than normal order can move the stock higher than you might want to pay at that time.

Better to buy $5,000 five times over the course of a month and ease your way into a position (more on this in "Understanding How To Execute Microcap Trades"). The stock may get cheaper in there, giving you a lower overall cost basis, but it might get a little more expensive, giving you a slightly higher overall cost basis. But don't sweat the difference between a $2.00 cost basis and a $2.30 cost basis; you're buying the stock in the "$2s" in expectation of holding for a couple of years and selling it in the "$10s."

And sell in pieces on the way out of a position too. If a stock becomes close to "fully valued," meaning you've got out of it about what you expected and the story hasn't gotten disproportionately better, beginning taking profits off the table.

When the 5,000 shares you bought at $3.00 becomes 5,000 shares trading at $7.00, sell 1,000 or 1,500 shares of your position if $7.00 is approaching your target. Reduce your risk while keeping part of your position to fully realize the projected upside. Sure, the stock might go to $9.00, but it also might go to $5.00.

Having said all that, if the story has changed dramatically for the better while you've been holding it, don't be afraid to "re-set" your price expectations and be prepared to ride it for all it's worth (while still taking money off the table occasionally), which leads us to . . . .

Rule #5 – Don't Trade Out Of Your Winners Just Because They're Winners

Another common mistake among would-be microcap investors is that they tend to want to sell out of their great buys too soon, after say, a nominal 15% gain on a stock they originally bought looking for a 3x or 10x return.

Don't shortchange yourself! Over the 20 years I've been active in microcap stocks, I've seen the tendency to sell a fast moving stock for a small gain. This often leaves you on the sidelines when really large moves occur. Some of the best performers in one period will often be a great performer in subsequent periods, a function of having bought great companies at great times at great prices.

Let leverage work in your favor – meaning that a stock that goes from $7 to $8 in a month, while an impressive return in the abstract, is a trifle compared to the fact that EACH dollar move in the stock provides you with that same 15% return on your original buy (if you buy 1,000 shares of a stock at $7 – a $7,000 investment – every $1 move higher is worth $1,000 to you, each of which represents a 15% gain on your original investment).

Bottom line: you can't own 100,000 shares of Microsoft today (value: $3 million) that you bought at a split-adjusted price of 25 cents (10,000% return) if you had sold the stock in 1990 for the 10% gain you got in a week. Money left on the table: approximately $2,975,000.

Through your research identify those stocks that can become your microcap "core holdings," stocks that are experiencing high growth themselves in high growth industries that you are likely to be able to hold on to them for many, many years, perhaps decades.

Acquire shares on a regular basis over time, building a meaningful, though not overly concentrated, position. Then through constant vigilance and monitoring, make sure that nothing changes about the story – meaning it's still cheap relative to its fundamentals on that day. As long as the micro (company) and macro (industry/ economy) story doesn't change, ride that winner until it is, itself, a blue chip.

Rule #6 – Don't Be Greedy

If a stock starts trading "out of whack" with its story and is higher than you know it ought to be, begin selling. You must have discipline here. I often preach "buy stocks for the long term, but be prepared to sell them in the short term."

If you've bought a stock at $3.00 with a price target of $10 and the story hasn't changed at all – in other words the company hasn't reached the milestones, or gotten the contracts, or gotten the approvals, or generated the sales you expected were necessary for the stock to reach your target – but it's already trading there anyway, sell it, or most of it.

By “most of it” I mean take 100% of your original investment plus a profit off the table and let the rest ride if you feel you must continue to own a position in the company in spite of it having traded above its inherent value.

For instance, if you buy 5,000 shares of a $1.00 stock with a target of $3.00 and it trades there ahead of its fundamentals, go ahead and sell at least 3,000 shares. This returns your principal and locks in an 80% profit ($4,000 on your original $5,000 investment). Then if the stock retreats to a price more in line with its fundamentals in the short term, you will have taken advantage of the short-term upswing and be ready to, potentially (if the stock is cheap relative to its fundamentals), buy the stock again! If the stock continues to run to, say, $5.00, so what? As Will Rogers said “you never go broke taking a profit.”

Most importantly, you’ve remained disciplined, which will serve you well in the end.

Here’s another horror story of how greed (or any other emotion such as fear or desperation for that matter) can ruin your day. A former business partner of mine bought 2,000 shares of MicroStrategy (NASDAQ: MSTR) at $19.00 – a very good price for the stock based on the company’s story and development at the time – hoping to double his money in a year, very plausible given the story.

One year later, the stock was trading at $308 per share, a 24x increase, and a good $250 more than the stock should have reasonably traded at based on reality – and perhaps most importantly, $270 more than his original price target and profit goal! I knew he was still holding it, and I called him (and one other friend) insisting that he sell the stock and take the money off the table, reminding him that the stock had performed better than his wildest dreams and was trading a ridiculously higher price than it should, given the facts.

His response was that he “knew it was going higher. I think it’s going to hit $310.” $310! He’s sitting with a $600,000 profit in a stock that had screamed up $295 per share and he’s holding out for $2.00 a share more! This was the height of hubris and greed, not to mention stupidity. (Of course, he had no tangible, measurable reason for thinking so; he just "felt it."). To which I responded, "okay, so sell just half of it and you'll bank a $295,000 profit and STILL own 1,000 shares."

He didn't. Five days later, the stock dropped to $185 in one day. I called him not to tell him I told him so but to plead with him to take money off the table (remember, on fundamentals the stock should have traded at maybe $50/share at the most generous of valuations). His response? "I can't sell it now; it's down almost half," forgetting or refusing to be satisfied that it was UP over 10x from where he bought it. All he could think about was the paper profits he had "lost" - once again, a purely emotional response no different from "I have a gut feeling it's going to $310").

To make a long story short, he rode that stock all the way down to $17/share without selling a share. He ending up finally selling the stock about five years later around $35/share, which was a little higher than his original target price, which he had hit – and then some! – just a few months after buying it in the first place.

Don't be greedy. Focus on the stock and price relative to your goals and the company's underlying story. When they get out of whack, you should be a seller.

Rule #7 – Don't Be Penny-Wise But Pound Foolish

I can't tell you how many times I've heard over the years, "I've got a limit order in at $5.60″ on a stock that's $5.65 Ask! (More on stock quotes and the "Ask" price later).

Think about this: you shouldn't even buy a microcap stock in the first place, unless you're in it for at least a triple (3x your investment) within a reasonable period of time, say two years. Note: a 3x return in two years is equivalent to about a 50% per year compound return – try earning that in CDs or an Index Fund!

If this is your purpose, then a nickel one way or another on the purchase price won't make a bit of difference. Don't be the "penny wise, pound foolish" type of investor here. If you see a $7 stock and think it should be trading as high as $10 NOW, don't nickel and dime your trade or put in unrealistic limit orders. Put in a limit order at ten cents or a quarter above the offer and get on with your life!

The same, of course, is true when you sell. If you have a large position to sell and the stock is relatively illiquid (trades less per day than the block you want to sell) then by all means enter a limit order to sell, just give yourself (and the market) some room by entering the limit slightly below the Bid price.

Whoever you trade through is required to get the best execution then can for you if they're acting as an agency (vs. a principal – more on that later), so you're going to get the best possible outcome in most cases anyway. What you absolutely don't want is to miss a selling opportunity by making it impossible for your trader to "work the block (of stock)" for you.

Yet another nightmare story: A very close friend of mine had worked for a tech company during the "dot com" boom and had acquired one million options to acquire shares at $0.25. Now he didn't buy these shares like you are doing as an investor, but the lesson is the same. Once the company did its IPO and he had held his options the requisite time, he exercised those options when the stock was at $1.00 (which was way overpriced as it was for this pre-revenue hope and a prayer company), giving him a $750,000 profit on the shares if he were to simply sell.

One million shares was a large block considering the trading volume of the stock, and he was correct in entering a limit order when he went to sell, but here is where he went wrong. The stock's Bid price was $1.00 and the Ask price was $1.05. He put entered his limit order to sell at $1.05! Why?! Keep in mind that the Ask price is the price at which existing shareholders are willing to sell their shares. The Bid price is the price at which people who currently don't own the stock are "bidding" to acquire shares – the Bid is where the buyers are; the Ask is where the sellers are, and he needed to be at or better than where the buyers were interested in acquiring the stock.

He could have made his limit at even $0.90 and still made a small fortune, and he should have. Instead, the stock softened, with the Bid-Ask dropping to $0.95 - $1.00. And even in the face of a weakening marketing he dropped his limit to not $0.95 but $1.00! He proceeded to chase the stock down to the point where his sell limit order was down to $0.50 but still at the Ask price! He was determined to get "max price" out of some ego-driven sense of not wanting to "lose" by selling at or under the Bid price. Within a year the stock – and the company – had collapsed; he never sold a single share.

Rule #8 – Do Pay Attention!

Small hiccups can have disproportionately large effects on small, thinly traded microcap companies. Regularly check up on what's going on with the companies you own shares in, ideally setting up news feeds to your e-mail accounts or using something as simple as Google Alerts to stay up to the minute on good and bad developments, developments that could provide sell signals, or even buying opportunities.

Since I've tortured you with horror stories thus far, which are real-life examples of the consequences of certain ill-advised approaches to investing in microcap stocks, I thought I'd share with you an accidental good outcome for a good friend who did not follow this Rule #7 to pay attention. Remember that this good outcome came completely from dumb luck, and that's not a strategy!

This friend of mine had invested a fair amount – I think it was $100,000 for around 100,000 shares - in an interesting tech company in the media space. It wasn't long after before the company experienced one trouble after another followed by a crisis, etc., and the stock plummeted – the never-to-recover kind of plummet it seemed.

My friend hadn't been paying attention through all of these trials and found himself with a stock he basically couldn't sell, or at least couldn't sell for anything more than cab fare somewhere! Better to hold on to it until the sale of shares could provide a capital loss to offset a capital gain one year. And that is what my friend did – simply ignored the company and the stock for years. Take the story up to hear as a cautionary tale and the lesson you should take away from it. Now on to his dumb luck!

Flash forward a few years, and I just happen to be sitting in his office chatting about something trivial when his phone rang. It was his former business partner, who had also bought a bunch of the stock at the same time and had similarly ignored it all the way down and was now just sitting on it. I knew Michael, so my friend put him on speakerphone. "Have you looked at XXX lately?" My friend hadn't. "It's at $8.35/share!" My friend went from having a worthless stock to a major six-figure winner in a matter of seconds.

I share this story with you only for its entertainment value, but also to highlight that, if you do your up-front work and evaluation correctly and dispassionately, even when you get one wrong – and you WILL get one wrong – they don't all stay that way permanently, as there are sometimes valuable pieces that someone is willing to buy or which provides the basis for a later investment from an outsider that turns the ship around on a seemingly sunken deal.

OTHER DUE DILIGENCE

What To Ask Management

After all the stocks have been screened and all the stories analyzed and all the numbers crunched, you still have only an "unanimated" list, a list with no life or luster. This is when we must pick up the phone and call management.

Your most likely target is the Chief Financial Officer (CFO). In smaller companies, you might even get the Chief Executive Officer (CEO) on the phone. In much larger companies you'll find a Vice President of Investor Relations whose job it is to speak to investors and answer their questions, but in most real opportunities among microcaps, you're looking to speak with the CFO or CEO.

Good CEOs care about how their stock trades (price, volume, shareholder breadth), not for the digits it adds to their personal bank accounts but for the currency it gives the company to make acquisitions, to raise capital on the most favorable terms, to attract talent with stock options that are meaningful, and, plainly, to appear more legitimate. Hence, microcap CEOs and CFOs, who are constantly struggling with thinly traded, undervalued shares, will talk to current and potential investors.

When you get them on the phone, you'll want to be prepared with some questions so as to be courteous with their time and effective in your fact finding. In general, you'd like to ask open-ended questions which allow for long and varied answers rather than close-ended ("yes" or "no") questions. You're looking for content and context, not just "what" but "why" and "how's it matter?" Keep in mind that an ethical CEO will necessarily confine his answers to that information which is already publicly available, but you can often read between the lines.

Sample Questions

- How long have you been with the company? (Context question: if he/she has been there only six months, your listening lens should be colored accordingly).
- Who is the most important department in your company and why (sales, finance, product development, marketing, R&D, etc.)?
- Do you feel that the market-cap represented by your shares represents a fair value for your company, and if not, why not?
- Do you like your job?
- If you had to put it into one sentence, what is the company's mission?
- What do you feel is the company's greatest point of differentiation in the market?

Research Competitors

Finance sites like Yahoo! Finance have a convenient tab that shows "Competitors," typically publicly traded companies. Clicking through to these competitors profile and SEC filings can often give you a treasure trove of information to ascertain your target's place in the industry, relative value and any competitive advantage and/or differentiators.

THOUGHTS ON THE PINK SHEETS

Many investors look at the Pink Sheets and the stocks trading there with a healthy amount of apprehension and/or skepticism, and not without some justification. "The Pink Sheets is daily publication compiled by the National Quotation Bureau (a private company not affiliated with the SEC or the Financial Industry Regulatory Authority, or FINRA) with Bid and Ask prices of over-the-counter (OTC) stocks, including the market makers who trade them. Unlike companies on a stock exchange, companies quoted on the pink sheets system do not need to meet minimum requirements or file with the SEC." (Investopedia)

The main technical difference between the Pink Sheets and other exchanges and markets is that Pink Sheet companies are not required to file periodic audited financials and otherwise provide "up to date" information to investors – like 8-Ks (material change notices), 10-Qs and 10-Ks.

The practical considerations include there typically being lower trading volumes in Pink Sheet shares and the requirement that investors wishing to buy most Pink Sheet-listed shares must complete a fair amount of paperwork that is meant primarily to acknowledge the risk of investing in lower-priced ("penny"), thinly traded securities. This extra hurdle tends to limit the pool of investors able to buy such stocks and leads to further illiquidity. Many investors just don't want the hassle, and many broker-dealers (where financial advisors and stockbrokers are licensed) don't want what they perceive is an increased liability that comes from allowing trades in such stocks.

Trading on the Pink Sheets does not mean necessarily that a stock is inherently more "risky" than those shares trading on other exchanges and markets. Issuers still must abide by the antifraud provisions of the Securities Act of 1933 – in other words, they can't lie just because they aren't filing regular reports with the SEC. Also, because the costs of being public and often exorbitant expenses associated with complying with auditing and reporting expenses of being "listed," many high-quality firms simply choose to trade on this low-cost platform.

This is especially true of local and regional companies (like banks) that want to offer at least nominal liquidity to investors in their companies but can't justify or refuse to spend the $400,000 minimum per year required to maintain a fully-reporting listing. Pink Sheets are also a popular place for large international companies listed on other global exchanges to have a cost-effective market in the U.S. where their shares or Advanced Depository Receipts (ADRs) may be quoted and listed.

One of stocks I referenced earlier – the one that I was sure was the most "conservative" and the "surest thing" of any stock I've recommended as an equities analyst – is a company called ePlus (NASDAQ: PLUS), a $300 million company – not a penny stock by any stretch and barely a microcap. I recommended ePlus at around $15 a share. I loved the company's sector, growth, business model, management, balance sheet – everything.

Not two quarters after I recommended the stock, the company decided to implement a fairly broad and involved restructuring/repositioning. Knowing that the even limited market (limited awareness and trading volume) at that time would likely punish the stock during this period of perceived uncertainty anyway, management decided to voluntarily delist from NASDAQ and trade on the Pink Sheets through the repositioning process, which ended up being a couple of years.

The stock traded down to $11 and stayed there for years, even as financial performance continued to be solid and the changes the company started to bear fruit. Note, that an investor who was keeping their eye on the ball – on the fundamentals – would not have been put off by the move to the Pink Sheets and the decline in stock price, because if it was a good buy at $15 – and it was – it was certainly a good buy at $11 if the fundamental hadn't deteriorated anyway. In fact, this disciplined investors would have seen this window as an opportunity to build a larger position at a lower average cost.

The moral of the story is that ePlus began trading back on NASDAQ and as of the date of this book's publishing trades at almost $90 per share, a 500% increase from my original recommend price and about 750% up from the buying opportunity the Pink Sheets-related price dip afforded.

Some other well-known international companies/brands that trade on the Pink Sheets are:

- Nestle (NSRGY.PK) is the world's biggest food and beverage company.
- Roche Holding Ltd. (RHHBY.PK) is a Switzerland-based company which is one of the largest pharmaceutical companies in the world.
- Volkswagen AG (VLKAY.PK) is the German car manufacturer which has the Volkswagen, Audi, Bentley, Bugatti, Lamborghini, SEAT, Skoda and Volkswagen Commercial Vehicles brands.
- Daimler (DDAIF.PK) is the parent company of Mercedes-Benz, the German automaker.
- BASF SE (BASFY.PK) is a German based chemical conglomerate known in past generations for audio tape and other "media" products.
- Bayer AG (BAYRY.PK), famous for its Bayer aspirin, is a producer of health products, agricultural products, and high performance materials.

This being said, investing in shares trading on the Pink Sheets requires that you perform an even higher level of "other due diligence" than you would need for a listed company since up-to-date and/or financial and other information is not always available on the company. Interviewing management and checking out the company's products and services becomes even more important.

THOUGHTS ON "TIPS"

Posts On Investor Boards and Your Friend-Of-A-Friend

Here's a virtual truism: if you - little old you (or me) - are getting a tip about a stock or reading about something related to a stock, then you can be almost certain that the "play" is over. This speaks to the idea of information arbitrage, which states that information which is poorly and/or narrowly distributed leads to pricing inefficiency – that is, a chance for unrecognized value.

So, in the context of a bulletin board post or a tip you've gotten from a friend of a friend, then information, by definition, is already more distributed and available that you typically want when looking for real value – a real discount to "inherent value."

I'm reminded of a twenty-something guy I used to work with. He was a very sharp, very ambitious young man who sat right next to me. He knew that I had deep experience with stocks and with really small stocks in particular, so he would pretty regularly lean around the corner and talk to me about his current and potential investments, even though our work at the time was unrelated to investments.

Not a week went by when he didn't have one stock or another that he had "heard something about" or "gotten a tip from a friend." All the stories were basically the same: "Steve, I heard from my friend 'X' or "I read on Yahoo!" that 'ABC Inc.' has 1) a new 'whichamajig' that is about to get approval' or 2) 'is about to get a huge order from Wal-mart' – pick a story.

The point is that by the time such a development in a company/ stock is in a public forum like Yahoo! (or any other bulletin board) or sufficiently deep into the rumor mill that a young, unconnected man like my friend was getting "tips," rest assured that there is no opportunity. The pros have played it and are now playing the rest of the public for fools, sadly a role that the general public is all too anxious to play.

Stay away from tips and postings and focus on real information, real fundamentals and relative value/discounted pricing.

SUMMARY

Let's recap how to approach investing in microcaps:

- Understand the difference between microcap and mainstream investing
- Understand why microcaps hold more upside and the additional risks they carry
- Get your head right – investing in microcaps requires a more patient, disciplined, non-trader approach to investing
- Do you research – do a thorough job, not stopping at a few data points that confirm some bias(es) that a particular stock might fit your microcap investing strategy
- Watch for land mines
- Incorporate the "tricks of the trade"
- Follow the Rules

Microcaps hold awesome potential to, at the least, boost the overall investment returns of your entire portfolio and in some cases may actually change your life.

ABOUT STEVE KANN

Stephen M. Kann is a 20-year veteran of the investment banking business, a serial entrepreneur, a venture mentor and microcap stock expert. He has personally originated more than $300 million in successful investment banking transactions. He has co-founded several companies, for which he has raised millions of dollars in investment capital, and some of which were exited through acquisition.

He is an advisor and mentor to start-up businesses and currently serves as a Mentor for AccelerateDC, a joint effort between the District of Columbia government and nationally recognized start-up accelerator, i-Corps.

His equity analyst credentials include having been the co-founder and editor of the Bull Market Microcap Review, one of the best performing stock newsletters in the country during the time of its publication and serving as a contributing analyst for Think 20/20, an independent equity research firm. His published stock picks have averaged more than 56% annually. Steve has been interviewed by, and quoted in, the Los Angeles Times, The Washington Times, Equities.com and other publications.

He has served as a host, moderator, panelist and speaker at multiple Consumer Electronics Association (CEA) conferences, including CES (the largest trade show in the world), CEA Innovate!, as well as at events by Foster.ly, AccelerateDC, 1776 and Tech Cocktail, usually in the role of capital markets expert.

Steve can be reached at steve@microcapmagic.com.

CASE STUDIES

The reports in the pages that follow will give the reader a glimpse into my thought processes as I match up the characteristics of each microcap stock with my microcap methodology as outlined in the book, as well as the particular rationale for each of my recommendations to buy.

The particularly astute reader may notice that, when I wandered even a little from my own rules (CMKG), the results were subpar as compared to the stock selections where I followed the rules strictly.

CASE STUDY: COACTIVE MARKETING GROUP

Here's why we love what we do: A stock trading at $3.70 that we think should be trading at $7 NOW -- and higher in the coming quarters. CoActive Marketing Group (CMKG, $3.70), is a full service marketing, sales promotion and interactive sales company that has shown great growth and seems to have plenty more upside to come. This undervalued company is involved in many of the leading edge marketing services in use in business today, including targeted ethnic marketing, event marketing, interactive new media, and e-commerce. In addition, the company is making inroads in providing its services to the lucrative Healthcare and Financial Services marketplaces, two segments that have been performing exceptionally well in a down economy.

The company reported some very impressive numbers for the third quarter, which we believe will catch the attention of the investor/analyst community. As is the philosophy of Bull Market MicroCap Review: More attention = More demand = More trading volume = Higher stock price.

What struck us most about CoActive Marketing Group is that during the worst three-year period the marketing/promotion industries have seen in decades, the company has held its own, deftly restructuring its cost infrastructure, and managing to come out of the other end of the doldrums actually GROWING. Net income for the quarter ending June 30th doubled, rising to $330,000, or $0.06 per share, from last year's $165,000. Sales for the quarter were $16 million, up 14% over last year's first quarter. That's the kind of growth we look for at Bull Market MicroCap Review, and the kind of increase which portends a nice potential jump in stock price over the next couple of quarters, if not sooner.

Why? Because the industries the company operates in are actually growing again. Consider the following trends: Spending levels had been hit so hard in previous years that, according to IEG, the main source of corporate sponsorship information, sponsorship spending alone by North American companies is expected to jump 9% in the coming year, to $9.4 billion. And in the 2003 a Promotion Trends study, co-sponsored by PROMO Magazine and the New York City-based Promotion Marketing Association, brand marketer respondents said that 57% of their marketing dollars went to trade or consumer promotion versus 38% that went to traditional advertising. Hammering home the future prospects of these specialized marketing niches, PROMO Magazine goes on to say, "A more telling indicator of the rising status of promotions as a strategic tool is the increasing involvement of CEOs. Brand promotion is where the brainpower is going these days, and CEOs, presidents and company owners are providing more of the juice needed for developing marketing that moves sales and enhances the brand." This is exactly what CoActive provides -- an extraordinary level of expertise in burgeoning fields of which few insiders at client companies have meaningful knowledge!

ETHNIC MARKETING -- A PROFITABLE NICHE AREA

This field is so big that it needs its own section in the newsletter! Marketing to ethnic groups -- especially first- and second-generation ethnic groups -- is a hidden opportunity that most marketers have long overlooked. But that's changing. Those who have paid attention, especially to the rapidly growing Hispanic population, have reaped big profits. Traditional marketing "wisdom" tells us to find a "sweet spot" demographic and put all our marketing dollars there. In other words, find out who has the most money to spend, and is most likely to spend it on what you have to offer, and gear your ads towards that audience. Companies like CoActive recognize the inherent limitations in such a strategy. Marketing efforts that are sensitive to various cultures and in the native languages of those cultures have proven time and again to be highly successful and very profitable.

It's worthwhile to have a look at the success other companies have been experiencing in this niche market. Two companies that target the Hispanic market (but don't compete directly with CoActive) are Hispanic Broadcasting (HSP, $29, down 2), and Global Payments, (GPN, $38, unch.). Global recently acquired DolEx Dollar Express for $200 million. DolEx is a consumer-to-consumer electronic money transfer company that provides services mainly to first- and second-generation US Latinos who wish to send money to friends and family in Latin America. DolEx has Western Union beat hands-down in the Hispanic communities, simply because they pay attention. By researching and focusing on this particular market, and allowing each center to act as a de facto gathering place and center for the Mexican immigrant community, they've cultivated a very loyal customer base. Hispanic Broadcasting, the largest Spanish language radio broadcasting company in the US, also saw good growth by taking this focus, increasing revenues 13% last quarter to $75 million (remember, this was a BAD year). The company, which owns 70 radio stations in the top Hispanic markets, also projects 12% year-over-year increases for the current quarter.

Through its MarketVision affiliate (of which CoActive is a 49% owner), CoActive delivers programs for its customers that specifically target and motivate Hispanic consumers. Market Vision has more than 20 years experience in marketing to the Hispanic community and has orchestrated many successful Spanish-language campaigns for high-profile clients. It's an opportunity that shouldn't be, and can't be, overlooked. There are 35 million Hispanics in the US today, and there will be at least

40 million by 2010. Four out of every ten new Americans are Hispanic, and, collectively, their purchasing power is immense. Since 85% of the Hispanic population is clustered in large population centers in 10 states, there are obvious opportunities there for targeted marketing. CoActive has become the leading specialist in targeting this influential community.

The advantage that MarketVision has over the competition is its focus and legitimacy in the Hispanic community. Originally, MarketVision was a small group, which CoActive founded and incubated, such that over the last few years, their business has gone from virtually zero to being a major force in Hispanic marketing. MarketVision is now the agency of record for Hispanic marketing for both Coca-Cola and Miller Beer, two excellent clients that provide them with good revenue streams, great growth markets, and good stability.

While Hispanic marketing is starting to take off, those agencies that take a "me too" approach (even much larger agencies like Saatchi & Saatchi) just don't seem to get it like CoActive gets it. In trying to cash in on the trend, larger agencies approach the market, but their approach doesn't ring true in that community. MarketVision was from the beginning a Hispanic company. As John Benfield, Chairman, President and CEO, explains it, "We incubated this group and made them (Hispanic professionals) the dominant and majority portion of the company. We made them the front end. Behind it, we put all of our conventional resources in such a way that it immediately gave MarketVision access to a 220 person company." MarketVision's clients have been responding well. MarketVision volume is building steadily, and this represents a major area of growth for CoActive Marketing Group going forward.

In addition, the company has broadened its platform of ethnic marketing services with the formation of Grupo Hacerlo, a network of affiliated Hispanic-owned and operated agencies that provide event and entertainment marketing services to Hispanic markets. Grupo Hacerlo is another tactical win for CoActive. In the Hispanic community, events are important, often more important than traditional print and television advertising. Many of the dollars devoted to Hispanic marketing go into event marketing. Remember the growth figure for sponsorship, above? The vast majority goes to event marketing. So picture spending growing by 9% within a fast-growing ethnic group, and you should get a picture of the explosion of great opportunities. Grupo Hacerlo, like MarketVision, is authentic. It's a network of small, independent, Hispanic-owned shops in cities around the country that have meaningful Hispanic populations. CoActive established a communication system to connect them all, and uses these groups for activation at the street- and community-level. This gives them the unique capability to run a national event promotion using local, culturally-sensitive resources, something CoActive's larger competitors simply cannot do.

HIGH-PROFILE CLIENT BASE

CoActive's client base is a virtual Who's Who of industry, with names including Schick, Coca Cola, Folgers, P&G, Valvoline, Disney, Corona, Old Navy, GM, Johnson & Johnson, and many more major firms that take the process of choosing a marketing agency very seriously.

Most recently, Diageo selected CoActive's US Concepts subsidiary as the agency of record to execute on-premise marketing for Diageo North America, and Diageo-Guinness USA brands in most states. Further, Schieffelin & Somerset, a joint venture between Diageo and LVMH Moët Hennessy Louis Vuitton also renewed its contract with US Concepts. We wouldn't be too far off base if we take the liberty to call CoActive the "champagne" of marketing organizations, especially as it becomes responsible for event marketing for leading brands such as Smirnoff, Captain Morgan, Bailey's Irish Cream, Guinness, Harp, Red Stripe, Johnnie Walker, Hennessy, Tanqueray, Grand Marnier, Moët & Chandon and Dom Perignon. We hope you'll join us in cracking open a bottle of the latter when CoActive's stock trades at what we believe is more reasonable levels, near the $6 mark.

CONTINUING RECOGNITION

CoActive was ranked the number four promotional agency for 2003 by PROMO Magazine, and ranked number one for its creative work. PROMO Magazine ranks the 100 best and brightest promotional agencies, ranking them for revenue results as well as the creative merits of their campaigns.

RECESSION PROOFING

It's important to note that over the last few difficult years, CoActive has performed well. During periods of economic pressure, advertising and marketing agencies are often the first to suffer. During such a time, a large company may feel the need to increase the bottom line by cutting the budget, and more often than not, that cut comes out of marketing, advertising and promotions. But, while making that cut, management realizes they have to deliver numbers, and will retain some of that cut to put it into something that is tactically promising and can deliver results they can count on. Usually, that means keeping tactical event marketing in the budget while other marketing and advertising dollars that have a longer-term strategy get the ax. Because the tactical event marketing and promotional activities in which CoActive specializes are the types of events that are kept in the budget while everything else is getting cut, CoActive can "weather the storm" better than other marketing organizations, and in fact, do better than most. And CoActive has proven this with three straight "up" years during these difficult times.

OPERATIONS AND SELECTED FINANCIALS

Now that we've covered the qualitative aspects of the business, let's peek at the nuts and bolts. Operationally, CoActive has held the line on expenses. And while operating expenses for the June 2003 quarter were $2.9 million, compared to $2.5 million in the year-ago quarter (up 15%), net income doubled in the same period. Over the last year, the company has right-sized itself by reducing headcount, eliminating redundancies between divisions, and focusing on keeping tight discipline over the budget. This rightsizing is largely over at this point, and the company seems to be right where it needs to be, in terms of size and operating efficiency, to provide a robust platform for further growth.

Much of CoActive's cost-cutting initiatives and focus on achieving greater efficiencies revolves around technology. In an interview we had with CoActive CEO John Benfield, he tells us, "We're a pretty technologically advanced company; that's part of our philosophy." One of the bright spots in a tough economy has been companies' increasingly creative use and leveraging of technology, and this has sparked an advancement in the kinds of technology-oriented marketing services CoActive provides, and that CoActive's management leverages for its own operational purposes.

CoActive has an improving balance sheet, with cash flow being used for both growing the business and shifting some short-term debt, which could constrain cash flow, to long-term debt over the last several quarters. Up to now, the company's deft use of leverage has allowed it to generate a ROE (return on equity) of over 12% in the last 12 months. That's a very good number in the current climate.

Although there are no immediate plans for acquisitions, Benfield notes that as growth continues to pick up, and as the company's currency, its stock, becomes more liquid and valuable, it will be on constant alert for new acquisition possibilities in this highly fragmented industry, an industry that the company is positioned to lead into the future.

KEY FINANCIAL DATA

Ticker Symbol:	**CMKG**
Recent Price:	**$3.65**
52 Week High:	**$3.70**
52 Week Low:	**$0.95**
Market Cap:	**$19 million**
P/E:	**10**
Price/Sales:	**0.29**
Fiscal Year:	**3/31**
Shares Outstanding:	**5.15 million**
Insider Ownership:	**18%**
Headcount:	**230**

MANAGEMENT

Led by CEO John Benfield since 1988, the company is in good hands. Unlike many other companies in the marketing and advertising business, there's no revolving door here. Members of the executive staff have a wealth of experience. Prior to joining CoActive, Benfield was Director of New Business at Colgate-Palmolive Company. For those of you who know your marketing, you know that consumer products powerhouse Colgate-Palmolive, along with others such as Proctor Gamble, are known as much for the MARKETING MINDS they produce as for the household brands they produce.

Also last year, CoActive was fortunate to appoint John Ward III as an independent member of its Board of Directors. Former CEO of American Express Bank, Ward is well known for his achievements in creating marketing concepts and implementing growth strategies both at American Express and in his previous career at Chase Manhattan.

PROSPECTS FOR GROWTH

The company has high expectations of continued growth, and looking at its aggressive strategies and key position in its markets, it's not hard to see why. As the company moves into high gear for the busy Christmas marketing season, we should see a higher stock price over the next quarter. The stock's growth pattern for the last year has been excellent, with no significant drops -- which underscores the fact that the company has a good backlog, a steady client base, and is staying closely on track with its strategies and goals for growth.

As we mentioned, fiscal fourth-quarter profits doubled year-over-year, and we see similar results when comparing fiscal year 2003 profits over fiscal 2002, with FY2003 profits at $1.8 million, up 95% over FY2002. Growth prospects for 2004 are excellent, with management anticipating earnings growth of between 25-30%. Fiscal 2004 EPS are projected to come in at $0.40-45, significantly higher (about 35%) than FY03's $0.32. At a 0.70 PEG ratio (a 0.70 PEG is where the PE multiple is 70%

of its earnings growth rate - in this case 25), that would mean a stock trading around $7. Next year it could mean a $10 stock price. And if the PEG expands to 1.0, which is very reasonable, we could see even better things next year.

SUMMARY

Promotional, ethnic, and other specialty marketing areas are growing fields, and in the face of a recovery, regardless of how weak that recovery may be, corporate expenditures on such marketing is on track to increase. Quite simply, it's where the results are. We look for this growth rate to increase as economic recovery continues, and we believe that the company is positioned for record growth in the quarters ahead.

This stock is on the verge of coming up on the radar screen of institutional investors, with virtually no shares owned by institutions. Lucky for Bull Market MicroCap Review subscribers, the stock still trades at a relatively anemic 11,000 shares per day (or just about $40,000 worth) on average, giving the stock a real chance to scream as visibility increases. We don't consider a MicroCap stock truly "discovered" until volume approaches $500,000 per day in sustained volume, and institutional ownership exceeds 25%, broadly distributed among several institutions. (Notice that the stock covered in our first issue, Collegiate Pacific (BOO $7.83) has only 8% of its shares in institutional hands).

This is a trend you'll see in our newsletter. No analysts cover this stock. Practically no one knows about this stock. But now, YOU DO!

EPILOGUE:

Coactive Marketing Group (CMKG) enjoyed a little bump in price after my initial recommendation but subsequently ran into management infighting and poor execution. The stock subsequently suffered an earned price reduction, but was ultimately acquired for a mere 33% loss (tiny compared to the outsize returns investment in microcaps can provide and more than made up for in the stocks outlined in the following pages, as you will see). In retrospect, CMKG was missing many of the things I think are important. There was nothing proprietary about the company, which, at best means increased competition and shrinking margins in the future, and at worst makes a company without deep pockets or other synergies a high-risk bet for bad news ahead. I strayed from my own rules on this one, as I got completely enamored with management, was a little overconfident in my assessment of the timing and utility of the service the company provided, and really just dove in with a deal that was deficient

CASE STUDY: COLLEGIATE PACIFIC

Collegiate Pacific is a sporting goods and equipment manufacturer/ distributor based in Dallas.

COLLEGIATE PACIFIC (BOO, $6.95) is the fastest growing factory-direct mail-order supplier of sporting goods and equipment to the institutional market (schools, churches, government agencies, etc.) in the United States. Collegiate Pacific has just increased its net income by 95% on an advancement of 24% in revenues (in the 9 month period ended March 31st) and is positioned for even greater growth over the next two years.

The company is on the verge of its biggest year ever, $21 million in revenue (FY June 30, 2003 estimated), up 29%, and EPS of 28-30 cents (estimated), up 58%. Earnings for the June quarter will be out imminently.

Virtually all of this growth to date has been realized internally, while several acquisition plays loom on the horizon. Pretty impressive, but really just par for the course for a management team that has accomplished the same thing twice before.

KEY FINANCIAL DATA

- Ticker Symbol:	BOO
- Recent Price:	$6.91
- 52 Week High:	$7.50
- 52 Week Low:	$4.15
- Market Cap:	$29 million
- P/E:	23
- P/Sales:	1.5
- PE/G:	0.6
- Yield:	1.2%
- Fiscal Year:	6/30
- Shares Outstanding:	4,300,000
- Insider Ownership:	68%
- Employees:	56

MANAGEMENT TEAM

When one looks to Collegiate Pacific, it is impossible to ignore the management team's 400 years of combined experience in the sporting goods and equipment industry. Before CEO Michael Blumenfeld founded Collegiate Pacific in 1998, in his first 25 years in the industry, he had successfully built from the ground up, two other sporting goods companies (BSN in 1972 and Sport Supply Group in 1991), an industry niche that he essentially created.

Add to the fact that both of these publicly traded entities grew from start-up to $100 million in annual revenues and it becomes evident that Collegiate Pacific's management team understands how to achieve improving revenue and operating profits. For good reason, Blumenfeld and crew are considered THE revolutionaries of this industry.

In fact, this management team has never had a down year in revenue in 31 years. You read that correctly -- not one. Collegiate Pacific, while similar in scale to the first two companies, is on pace to reach that same $100 million threshold, albeit at a quicker pace.

Furthermore, it should be comforting for a potential investor that Collegiate's management's interests are wrapped up in the company. Insiders own 68% of the outstanding shares, thus their interests are vested in the company's success.

Add to this the fact that Collegiate Pacific employees recent voted to receive profit sharing instead of annual cash bonuses, and it becomes apparent that the entire group has an incentive to maximize shareholder value.

Finally, a succession plan is in good hands. Adam Blumenfeld, the son of CEO Michael, has over 10 years of industry experience, and is currently the President.

COMPETITION

A powerful variable worth emphasizing when choosing a MicroCap equity investment is the existence of a competitive advantage. In the MicroCap market, survival and expansion is often dependent on a steep barrier to entry derived from intellectual property, goodwill, customer captivity or economies of scale exist.

In the sporting goods and equipment industry, the absence of a barrier to entry leads to a bevy of small companies that, at best, merely survive, but typically vanish as quickly as they emerge. Fortunately for Collegiate Pacific's shareholders, Blumenfeld has learned the methods by which the firm has established a competitive advantage in a highly competitive, yet stagnant market.

Though its smaller competitors face little to no barrier to entry, and its larger challengers possess greater capital, name recognition and customer base, the majority of the sporting goods and equipment industry has been mired in mediocrity.

Over the past three years, the industry at large has meandered across a $4 billion plateau, making few moves towards improvement. However, despite overall malaise in the industry and a retreat of the overall economy, Collegiate has remained an anomaly.

While its competition is mostly regional, Collegiate Pacific has acted on the lessons accrued through lifetimes in the industry. Executives have learned how to surpass regional competition, and leap over industry stalwarts, to become the fastest growing sporting goods and equipment manufacturing and distribution company in the country.

Currently, management anticipates that Collegiate Pacific will continue to grow internally at an astounding annual clip of better than 25%-30% -- a figure that can be attributed to a comprehensive service offering, an aggressive marketing campaign, and an exponentially increasing customer base. And this gives does not factor in revenue and earnings growth derived from acquisitions, many of which are contemplated.

PROPRIETARY PRODUCTS AND DISTRIBUTION

In order to remain competitive in the sporting goods/recreation industry, Collegiate's management has discovered the need to provide a one-stop shop for a customer's needs. Whereas potential competitors either only distribute, or have minimal manufacturing capability, Collegiate not only maintains an enormous marketing and distribution capacity, but it is also an ambitious manufacturer of its own proprietary sporting goods and equipment. Hence, overall margins dwarf those of competitors.

Currently, Collegiate manufactures over 500 of its own products, which contribute more than 40% of its annual revenue. Since the company earns more from the sales of its own products, Blumenfeld & Co. have been determined to develop more of their own products (bleachers, balls, weight lifting equipment, various goals, posts, volleyball standards and tunnels), to increase such products' contribution to the revenue mix.

Furthermore, the company derives revenues from strategic alliances. Collegiate Pacific maintains distribution rights for sports equipment from companies like Markers (field markers), Funnel (portable soccer equipment), Edwards, (tennis marketing/distribution), Equipment, Inc. (tennis accessory equipment), Mark One (camping equipment), and Diamond (baseball), adding both name brand recognition and revenues.

Moreover, a substantial portion of Collegiate Pacific's growth has been through its proprietary, non-branded products. Essentially, management is in the process of mirroring a strategy employed at Sport Supply Group, in which it places name-brand insignias and logos on no-frills, proprietary products. In 1991, by buying the rights of MacGregor, Sport Supply Group -- Blumenfeld's 2nd company -- attached the MacGregor name onto generic proprietary products, creating over $40 million in sales over a 6-year period.

With Collegiate Pacific's present offering of 2000+ generic products, its current alliances promise to pay substantial dividends. In fact, we understand that Collegiate Pacific is always on the lookout for a deal to acquire the rights to a major brand, several of which might be available if the right deal can be made. This could be very big if and when it happens.

While its service offering is impressive, the Company's speed to market and its ability to distribute its products quickly, marks another variable responsible for the rapid expansion of revenues and institutional customers.

Collegiate offers the fastest shipping turnaround in the industry. Collegiate guarantees a 2-day delivery for all its manufactured products whereas the industry standard remains a sluggish 3-6 weeks! This huge differentiator has allowed the company to attract new customers in large numbers. By adding 1000 customers a month, the company has experienced six straight years of revenue growth, with profits accelerating faster than overall revenue -- a sign of tremendous operating leverage.

The speed with which Collegiate Pacific delivers its own goods has improved the mix of its own products as a percentage of sales by 100% over the past 18 months. This figure stands to improve even more with strategic acquisitions.

MERGERS AND ACQUISITIONS

Acquisitions since 1998

Product Merchandising: Mail order distribution company distributing products and equipment for summer camps

Vantage Products International: Distributor of baseball netting and baseball related products

Mark One: Distributor of camping and sporting goods

Kesmil Manufacturing: Manufacturer of a broad line of athletic equipment

Michael Blumenfeld has been called "one of the biggest dealmakers you've never heard of" by a mergers and acquisitions specialists on the Street. One tool for generating new revenue he has used over the course of his steady and successful career has been the strategic (and mostly successful) acquisition of over 120 companies.

At Collegiate Pacific, Blumenfeld still employs this acquisition philosophy to broaden the firm's product offerings. Collegiate is very disciplined and understands the importance of due diligence, legal counsel and credit history. While Mr. Blumenfeld always keeps around "12 companies on the radar screen" for acquisition purposes at all times, he is experienced and knowledgeable enough to know a good deal when he sees one.

The company is just as likely to strike a deal at any moment with any or all of the 3-5 companies he keeps at a "can do at almost any time" level, and management is disciplined enough to pull out of a deal if it isn't a perfect fit, AND accretive to earnings.

The sports equipment industry is currently involved in a large-scale consolidation. Mainstays in the field such as Wilson and Spalding are primary involved in the retail space, while Riddell, MacGregor and Rawlings have advertised their availability for sale.

Collegiate Pacific stands to benefit from the consolidation of at least one of these companies into the Collegiate Pacific direct selling model. For a potential investor, it is important to understand that the management squad has a spectacular record with M&A and is determined to make accretive acquisitions over the next 24 months.

While growth by M&A is not necessary for Collegiate Pacific to enjoy sustained profitability and internal growth, executives expect to acquire anywhere from 2-4 important companies that would contribute substantially to organic revenue by fiscal year 2004. The company possesses the financial strength, operating platform and experience to acquire some of the most recognized companies in the sporting goods and equipment industry.

STOCK PRICES AND EARNINGS EXPECTED TO RISE

The firm is moving favorably against the grain. With former industry titans crumbling due to operational and financial difficulties, Collegiate Pacific continues to refine its best practices and industry-best balance sheet, and to draw upon its experience and operating leverage. The management team has been working an effective growth and M&A strategy for over 25 years, and the third time is likely to be equally, if not more of a charm.

Although M&A activity stands to improve Collegiate Pacific's financial results, executives believe that its internally driven operations will produce more than $3 million in income on a $40 million sales run-rate in the current fiscal year. The estimated $.75 EPS on 4.3 million outstanding shares should justify a substantial increase in the price of the stock. With its organic growth of 1000+ customers a month, coupled with imminent strategic acquisitions, Collegiate is expected to come close to doubling its 2003 revenues and earnings in fiscal 2004.

Currently, the stock stands at $6.95 per share, a mere 13 times FY 2004 estimated EPS. The company is presenting at the Roth Capital Conference in NYC in September. Don't be surprised to see a double or better here over the next 12 months, as institutions and the rest of the investing crowd discovers this gem and bids the stock up to what we believe is a more reasonable $10-12 per share in the nearer term and higher yet over the coming 12 months or so. (After all, WE have just discovered it!!)

Oh, and by the way, the stock pays a 1.2% dividend while you're waiting for the stock to appreciate -- not terribly exciting, but better than many of today's money markets!

Financial Disclosure: Steve Kann owns 9000 shares. Todd Shaver owns none. No other employee of BullMarket.com owns shares. This may change in the future, of course, but not until at least next week. We wish you to have the first opportunity to acquire shares.

EPILOGUE:

I recommended Collegiate Pacific (BOO) twice over six years (you'll see it below under Sport Supply Group, a company it later acquired).

It took six years for the first recommendation to pay off (a 127% return, working out to 14% annualized) but only nine months to pay off the second time (more than 100%), which reinforces one of the themes of the book that, while it may take a while, the market always recognizes value eventually; we just have to have the courage and discipline to focus on the fundamentals of each company relative to price and wait for the "crowd" - the broader market - to catch up.

CASE STUDY: DIALYSIS CORPORATION OF AMERICA

The most recent gem unearthed from the Bull Market MicroCap mine is a booming company immersed in an explosive industry -- Dialysis Corp. of America (DCAI, $5.90).

Founded in 1976, the Florida-based company develops and operates outpatient kidney dialysis centers in select locations across the United States. The centers function to provide dialysis and ancillary services to patients specifically suffering from chronic kidney failure -- generally referred to as end stage renal disease, or ESRD.

Our endorsement of Dialysis is based upon the company's clean and improving balance sheet, an impressive growth strategy, and the fortuitous position of being in an industry sector poised for rapid expansion with the aging of the "Baby Boomer" population.

EMERGENCE

Through its 26 years experience in developing and operating dialysis treatment facilities, the company carved a niche in the Healthcare industry by providing acute inpatient dialysis treatments under contractual relations with hospitals and medical centers in areas serviced by outpatient dialysis.

To cater to a different sub-segment, management began a homecare, or method II, home patient treatment. This service, which is run by a wholly owned subsidiary -- CDA Medical Services -- provides equipment and supplies, training, monitoring and follow-up assistance to patients who are able to perform their treatments at home. Recognizing that it had hit on a huge vein of opportunity, the company began in 1995 what has become a rapid expansion strategy. The company went public a year later.

INDUSTRY OVERVIEW

Before we plunge into the qualitative and quantitative rationale behind our advocacy of Dialysis, it is important to grasp an overview of the industry in which it operates.

Kidneys are our bodies' filtration system. They remove harmful substances and excess water from our blood, enabling our bodies to maintain proper and healthy balances of chemicals and water. Chronic kidney disorder, or ESRD, emerges when there exists a chemical imbalance and buildup of toxic chemicals -- creating a disease characterized by advanced irreversible renal impairment.

A likely consequence of complications resulting from diabetes, hypertension, advance age and specific hereditary, cystic and urological diseases, ESRD can be treated either by kidney transplant, or through regular dialysis treatments lasting for the rest of the patient's life.

Based upon this need, 4,200 dialysis facilities have been built across the United States to provide dialysis -- and there are not enough of them. Companies such as Dialysis have endeavored to treat those infected with ESRD through various dialysis treatment methods.

While kidney transplants provide the most immediate fix to a kidney disorder, the limited number of available kidneys for transplant makes dialysis through hermodialysis -- which is performed through an artificial kidney -- the most popular treatment. Hermodialysis can be conducted from an outpatient facility, inpatient hospital facility, or a patient's home.

In fact, over 80% of ESRD patients receive their treatments through non-hospital-owned outpatient dialysis centers. Consequently, those companies -- like Dialysis -- that are intelligent and able enough to cater to this rising demand will benefit handsomely.

THE ECONOMICS OF DEMOGRAPHICS

The qualitative aspects of Dialysis Corporation of America that warrant buying shares begin with the company's position in an industry poised for rapid expansion.

According to the Center for Medicare and Medicaid Services (CMS), treating ESRD in America's 286,000 affected people costs $22 billion annually. The CMS also suggests that this figure stands to increase substantially with the aging of the baby boomer generation.

Even without the contribution of the baby boomer generation, incidence of ESRD has DOUBLED in each of the last three decades. However, the first wave of baby boomers will begin reaching 60 years of age in two years, and by 2010, 117 million Americans will be over that age. A surge in age-related disease, notably ESRD, is coming.

Furthermore, a large percentage of ESRD is seen in diabetics. With 33% of America's adult population now tipping the scales as chronically obese -- a known cause of adult onset diabetes -- the cases of ESRD brought on by diabetes through obesity are likely to swell considerably.

Moreover, as more children weigh in as chronically overweight, they too will be subjects of Type I and Type II diabetes. These facts place dialysis providers on the leading edge of an unfortunate trend. Based upon these developments, we are confident that Dialysis maintains the personnel and fiscal criteria necessary to exploit the present opportunity created by an aging population.

MANAGEMENT STRATEGY AND OVERVIEW

A favorable qualitative aspect behind the company is the tight ship run by the firm's management. Based upon its 26 years of experience, the company's management has seen it all, and understands how to grow effectively and efficiently.

Recognizing that the company has the unique opportunity to grow alongside an upswing in demand for dialysis treatment, over the past few years the company has made significant advancements in its service offerings and physical expansion.

Since the company relies on a greater number of operating facilities to augment revenue, management has expanded operations through independent development, acquisitions, and strategic alliances. The company maintains relationships with nine hospitals, and is continuing to seek and negotiate with individual physicians and others to establish new outpatient dialysis facilities.

In Q102, Dialysis opened a center in Pennsylvania, and in the second quarter of that year, a new center in Georgia. In February 2003, two more centers were constructed in Ohio and Maryland, and the company is in the development stages for two new centers -- one in Indiana and the other in Virginia.

While this expansion has been impressive, this success is particularly intriguing because it has occurred with very few, albeit effective, acquisitions. While acquisitions tend to come with existing technology, patients and physicians -- all invaluable variables in a rapidly growing industry -- they are costly, and carry a significant risk of default.

Consequently, management has primarily developed its own dialysis centers from the ground up, in addition to taking minority and majority stakes in many existing dialysis centers.

Decisions like these have ensured that Dialysis's management has the long-term health of the company in mind ---a telltale sign of a long term, value-driven investment.

FINANCIAL COMMENTARY

On the financial (quantitative) side of things, Dialysis is sizzling. What is most important to concentrate on here is the revenue figure. Dialysis is in an extremely competitive industry, and is investing in its own future NOW, taking advantage of low interest rates and surges in cash flows to invest in new revenue streams. For example, by virtue of recent additions in Pennsylvania and in Georgia, the company's revenue in 2002 increased 33%, or $6.3 million, over 2001.

Over the past three years, revenues have increased over 50% annually, compared to the rest of the industry's 25% growth. Furthermore, operating income advanced 64% from 2001 to 2002, as old dialysis centers matured, and new centers were added.

While the increase in net income ($1.2 million in 2002 -- an increase of $400,000 over 2001) has trailed the growth rates of revenue and operating income, this is because new properties are still in developmental stages, and extra cash is being invested in future expansion -- hardly a negative omen! That expansion is paying off; as the six months ended June 30th, 2003 saw revenues grow 20% over the same period in 2002.

Through its forged alliances, internal development, and strategic acquisitions, the company currently operates 16 outpatient dialysis centers across the east. Each of these branches has added significant revenues to the company's operations, and added fuel for the company's future growth.

Worth noting, in 2002, growth in total treatments advanced 18%, and same center revenues grew a substantial 22%. Moreover, the acquisition of the Georgia facility added 4% in revenues and 5% in operating income. These figures show that the development of newly acquired facilities is progressing effectively and efficiently.

As negotiations progress with more hospitals and physicians around the country, Dialysis's expansion will likely be more effective. By investing in new properties, the company is positioning itself well for the increasing demand for dialysis centers.

PERFORMANCE METRICS

While taking a financial snapshot of the company suggests that Dialysis is operating well, by analyzing a few key financial metrics we comfortably determined that the company's shares are undervalued. Surveying the price to book ratio, we can see that DCAI is trading at 1.9x book, whereas the remainder of the dialysis industry is trading at 3.6x book.

Based upon the aggressive growth strategy, we believe that the company's recent investments in its future should propel shares to the level of the remainder of the industry.

Then there's that growth. The company's shares trade at only 21 times its trailing 12 months' earnings. While earnings haven't kept up with the company's blistering sales growth of more than 50% per year, due to the company's commitment to investing today to take advantage of powerful trends in the industry, we're confident in projecting that earnings growth will inch its way toward, and then pass, revenue growth as the company begins to take full advantage of the economies of scale it is building.

As earnings accelerate, look for a "double hit" of higher earnings per share and shares trading at a higher multiple of earnings.

Picture this: The company doubling earnings over the next 24 months to around $0.50 per share and the stock's multiple catching up with the company's growth.

However, let's not even be that bold, but rather say it trades at 30 times earnings. At $0.50 a share, a 30x multiple would put the stock in the mid teens. That's how we see it. Right industry; right time; right expansion approach; right management.

KEY FINANCIAL DATA	
Ticker Symbol:	DCAI
Recent Price:	$5.90
52 Week High:	$5.90
52-Week Low:	$2.75
P/E:	21
Price/Book:	1.9
Price/Sales:	0.7
Market Cap:	$23 million

SUMMARY

We believe Dialysis is an optimal MicroCap pick not only because its shares are undervalued and positioned for growth, but also because of the company's ambition to expand, and its overall fiscal discipline necessary to achieve that development.

Dialysis happens to be in an industry positioned for long-term and powerful growth. Fortunately, for shareholders, the company is beginning to come into its own at the perfect time.

The firm has expanded aggressively, but don't think for a moment that it has completed its development. New dialysis centers will be opened over the next few months. More importantly, they will be opened in a manner and at times that will maximize and boost future earnings.

Don't be scared off by the stock trading at its 52-week high. A lot of stocks are trading at similar levels right now. This to us is just proof positive that investors are beginning to come out of their bunkers and are looking for strong growth plays trading at relatively low multiples.

Sometimes, it pays to position oneself in front of an unstoppable trend. A mentor of ours once referred to this as "digging a hole in front of a charging elephant." The elephant in this case is the relentless march of an aging, increasingly obese population, and the attendant health problems like kidney disease. The hole you can dig is a bucket of shares in Dialysis Corporation of America. You can worry later about how to eat the elephant!

EPILOGUE:

Dialysis Corporation of America (DCAI) is one of my favorite picks of all time. It was so clear in evaluating the company that it should be a big winner, and it was.

It had everything, superb management, strong macro growth in its space and strong internal growth and profitability. I recommended DCAI at $2.95 (split-adjusted) and it was acquired in less than seven years for $22.50, making it one of my biggest single winners ever.

CASE STUDY: ePlus

Our third installment of the Bull Market MicroCap Review features a company that probably has one of the biggest market caps we'll cover here. And we think the current market cap is a fraction of where it will be in the coming quarters.

ePlus (PLUS, $15.09) is a developer, vendor and financier of information technology (IT) and other assets. Through its enterprise cost management software model, ePlus assists middle market and larger businesses, governments and institutions to organize, implement, control and maintain cost savings methods, through money-saving alternatives.

But don't mistake ePlus for a pure technology company, susceptible to the whims and inherent volatility of a fickle marketplace. ePlus is the perfect modern hybrid -- a company that leverages powerful technology to perform highly valuable and, in some cases, very low-tech services for customers, but in a more effective and efficient way than ever possible before.

At the most basic level, the company derives revenues from its financing activity, arranging financing plans for customers to lease or buy IT assets. Financing inherently creates customers where there weren't any before -- customers that don't necessarily have the capital for all-cash purchases. However, on a more sophisticated level, ePlus has developed or acquired proprietary technologies designed to facilitate the requisition, order approval, tracking and product reporting, through the use of Internet, email and other IT devices, to automate the procurement process.

The impressive result has been that, in a down economy like the one we're in, especially in hard-hit sectors like the moribund IT hardware business, ePlus has made it possible for customers to do more with less, and has reduced its own cost structure in the process.

This has allowed ePlus to be one of the only companies in the space to increase earnings every year during the 3 1/2-year downturn -- to $10 million over the last 12 months -- even while suffering a considerable drop in revenue during the worst of it.

PRODUCTS

The company has the philosophy that the cost management space has traditionally been accessible to a select few, and by simplifying the process, the "ePlusSuite" will win over the hearts and minds of a significant chunk of its target demographic of 60,000 midsize companies.

ePlusSuite's proprietary products improve a company's efficiency by enabling its management to control the procurement and allocation of high-tech equipment from a centralized location. To illustrate how ePlus serves its customers, we describe one of the company's offerings here.

First, under its Procure+ software solution, ePlus improves supply-chain productivity by utilizing electronic catalogues, order tracking, workflow and business tools. The Procure+ suite was added through acquisition in 2000, and was modified to facilitate and streamline the procurement process.

Second, Finance+ re-uses the detailed asset information from Procure+ orders and assets to originate and produce leasing schedules, and populate pre-negotiated lease documents. The automation accelerates financing, and, by leasing, customers gain a tax write-off of up to 100% of the amount financed.

The company delivers its business model based on the notion that any organization or company is a perpetually evolving entity, seeking new ways to improve efficiency, cut time and reduce costs in the procurement process. As customers begin to see an upswing in business spending, the momentum of the cost management industry is expected to grow correspondingly.

Companies are likely to invest in cost management technologies such as ePlusSuite in order to strengthen their positioning during periods of economic growth, and to mitigate the effects of the next recession.

PERSPECTIVE ON A WIDER ECONOMY

In order to fully appreciate the recent performance of ePlus, one must consider the broader context in which it has been achieved. In short, the company is one of our favorites because it has demonstrated the ingenuity to retain profitability despite the dotcom and overall Tech implosion since 2000.

Rather than following the herd of tech stallions that brandished the growth-without-restraint mantra of the late 1990s, ePlus has defined itself as marcher to a different drumbeat -- that of profitability. Larger competitors with established backgrounds like Commerce One and IBM stole the spotlight during the late 1990s, while ePlus engaged in quiet and strategic acquisitions, and superior research and development.

However, as we now know all too well, investing in high-tech (or any industry for that matter) is foolish when there is minimal historical precedent, and equally as important, an invisible or slapdash business plan.

When an economy is flattened by a recession, businesses often pinch their technology expenditures tightest until a rebound is perceived as sustainable and substantial. Regardless of this reality, history has been rather kind to IT. In 1985 and 1990, economy-wide Tech spending decreased by 5%, but the spending climate fully recovered within 6 quarters. Unfortunately, the tech bubble burst louder in 2000 than any other IT explosion in history, and spending still hasn't rebounded.

With the advent of the recession of 2001, the glamorous high-growth (and debt-laden) companies responsible for the Nasdaq's climb, relinquished their big market capitalizations in a few short months. Between Q401 and Q202, tech spending dropped off 15%, and now, 2.5 years later, a recovery still remains elusive.

Technology factories in Q202 were only producing at around 62% of their operating capacity, and still remain far below the 75-80% margin -- an unofficial threshold in the technology industry considered necessary to attain in order to build pricing strength, and increase earnings.

The companies that withstood the tech fizzle have come to realize that survival is dependent on comprehensive and swift financial restructuring. However, success has been hard to come by, as even the most adaptive of these companies were lucky to see a quarter or two of profitability during the tepid investment climate.

One beacon of light during these dark days has been ePlus, which has not seen its earnings in the red for over five years, and has grown earnings in each of the last two.

Rather than outshining others through combative marketing, ePlus reengineered and refocused its own functionality to gain a strategic competitive advantage, and improve its revenue mix. While many companies have sat back and awaited the end to the tech-spending drought, ePlus has been proactive, focusing on its strengths and dedicating itself to improved profitability.

Now, with the overall Tech industry beginning what many consider a sustained upswing, ePlus is positioned for even greater growth and profitability, and, we believe a corresponding surge in stock price.

STRONG FINANCIAL PERFORMANCE

As the economy in general and the Tech sector in particular rebound, it's important to get to the "what" and "why" in ePlus's remarkable performance.

For the quarter ending June 30th, ePlus announced another quarter of sound earnings. The company enjoyed a year-over-year earnings increase of 17% to $2.3 million, from $2 million compared to the same quarter in 2002, on about a 10% jump in revenue to $80 million. Earnings per share improved from $0.19 to $0.24. Overall revenue from the trailing 12 months came in at about $300 million versus just over $200 million for 2002.

These numbers become even more impressive when one considers that overall IT spending in the last year was flat. We expect continued earnings growth running ahead of revenue growth over the next two years.

The Darwinian logic of business suggests that it's not the strongest, but the most adaptive that survive. Despite losing $102 million in revenues between 2001 and 2002, ePlus calmly adapted, reengineering its cost structure and modifying its revenue mix. At the end of fiscal 2002, this strategy actually improved earnings 7% from $8.3 million to $8.9 million between 2001 and 2002.

Notwithstanding the longest and deepest slump in Tech history, ePlus managed to defy the odds by creating an efficient operating system focused on its strengths and most profitable product lines. Recognizing that the company's reliance on sales and financing of information technology and other assets results in sales volatility, management redirected the company towards the avenues generating the most revenue.

While management blames the decline in sales from those years on the overall economy, ePlus's improved profitability can be attributed to a plan designed to mitigate earnings volatility. As part of the restructuring, ePlus shifted from the high-dollar, lower-margin revenue product lines -- such as sales from equipment and sales of leased equipment, which declined 45%. In its stead are high-margin, lower dollar revenue services, like lease revenue fees and software fees, which increased 21% during the downturn. Management has stated its intention to continue to concentrate on its highest margin revenues, such as those from fees and other income, which increased 39% to a record $19 million in the last fiscal year.

FINANCIALS

There is much to like about ePlus's financials. As of June 30, 2003, the company had $24 million in cash ($3 per share) and overall book value of $112 million (over $12 per share), $92 million of which was tangible assets. The company's quick ratio (current assets/current liabilities -- basically a company's ability to meet short term obligations on a moment's notice) was a very healthy 2:1.

This means that PLUS trades at 1.2x book. As a comparison, let's look at quasi-comparables from the sectors in which ePlus operates. Ariba (ARBA, $3.17), the most prominent stand-alone procurement software company, trades at 4.3x book and yet lost $244 million in the year ended June 30th, 2003. In fact, ePlus generated more revenue than Ariba over that period! Yet Ariba's market cap is $850 million and its losses exceed its revenue!

Such is the continuing optimism that surrounds companies that promise streamlined procurement and cost management solutions. ePlus provides all that and more, offering its customers the financing to back the IT assets acquired through the supply chain. The closest overall analogous business is Hypercom (HYC, $5.38), which sells and finances equipment solutions, but in the highly specialized area of credit card processing equipment, making the company's revenue far more narrow and volatile.

Hypercom also lacks any technology platform that distinguishes it in the way ePlus does. Hypercom has lost scads of money in every year since 2000 (more than $39 million in the most recent year) but still commands a stock price that is 1.4x book, in spite of lower growth prospects than a highly diversified company such as ePlus.

KEY FINANCIAL DATA	
Ticker Symbol:	PLUS
Recent Price:	$15.09
52 Week High:	$16.06
52-Week Low:	$6.04
Market Cap:	$140 million
PE:	15
Price/Revenue:	0.50
Fiscal Year:	3/31
Shares Outstanding:	9.5 million
Insider Ownership:	20%
Employees:	650

ANTICIPATED GROWTH

Recent CIO Magazine's Tech Poll results indicate that 12-month forward spending plans for IT are now at 6% over last year and, according to First Call, 9% for 2004. By the end of 2005, analysts estimate total IT spending to advance by a further 15%, due to the improved economic climate and the need to replenish inventory supply.

The poll also concludes that these expectations are skewed by the high increases projected by smaller firms -- ePlus's target market -- which expect IT spending to increase an average of 16%. Large firms were surveyed at a much smaller increase of 1.5%. ePlus is positioned firmly in front of the wave of the greatest expected growth, and we expect that ePlus will comfortably outperform overall industry revenue growth and will improve its earnings at the high end of an annual 20-25% estimate.

While it is logical that a company that has already performed well during an anemic spending climate would improve its earnings in an economic rebound better than competitors who have failed to do so, the use of projection illustrates a science to our assumptions.

Using a forward-looking PEG ratio, based on ePlus's projected 20-25% a year earnings growth, we can determine that, at the current PE, PLUS will have a PEG range of 0.5-0.7 based on FY04 (ending March 31, 2004) numbers. At either end of this range, the prospect of significant price appreciation is great.

With the PEG ratio, the lower the ratio the better, because it shows that earnings growth is outpacing the premium being paid on that growth. In the case of ePlus, the current share price is not consistent with the level at which the company expects to perform.

Of course, the company might NOT perform as we expect, but, given the way it has performed in a down economy, we're comfortable that it will. The current price of ePlus seems like a bargain to us, and we expect it to increase accordingly.

MANAGEMENT

ePlus has shined so brightly because of its strong management. Its management strategy and execution during these trying times has been more than impressive. By tinkering with his company's product lines and streamlining its cost structure, CEO Phillip Norton has improved the company's revenue mix, despite confronting one of the greatest industry-wide downturns in Tech history.

Norton joined the company in March 1993 and has served since that time as chairman of the board and chief executive officer. He focuses specifically on company strategy, e-commerce execution, partnerships, and overseeing the sales and marketing arm of the business. Norton is an accomplished entrepreneur who has successfully managed large companies. Systems Leasing Corporation, which he founded in 1978, was sold to PacifiCorp in 1985. At the time of his departure in 1990, PacifiCorp held assets of over $800 million and was one of the largest third-party lessors in the country.

Bruce M. Bowen has been in the specialty finance business since 1982 and founded ePlus in 1990. He serves as the company's executive vice president, as well as president of ePlus Group, its leasing company subsidiary responsible for Finance+. Bowen has over 20 years of finance industry experience and is an expert in federal and municipal government finance.

SUMMARY

Demand is first beginning to pick up for cost management software in medium-sized business -- the demographic ePlus targets. As companies begin to grow, they will need more inventory, technology and assets -- creating a greater need to engage a system to manage those purchases.

As with the previous two stocks that we have profiled, Collegiate Pacific and CoActive Marketing, this company has received minimal analyst coverage, and subsequently has maintained modest trading volume. But we have a strong sense that such analyst coverage is coming at some point soon, and we anticipate that the interest in, trading volume, and share price of ePlus will rise accordingly.

We think that ePlus and its shares are ready for a few strong years. The market has just started to agree with us over the last week or so, bidding the stock up from around \$12 to its current \$15 level, but far short of its all time high of \$57 -- lofty heights that the stock might well see again given its strong competitive positioning and the expected surge in IT purchasing and financing activity over the next few years. But we would never predict such a price move -- quite yet. We see revenue and earnings growth justifying a price closer to \$20 by year-end 2003 and \$25-30 by the end of 2004, making \$15 look like a good value to us.

EPILOGUE:

This was another wild ride. ePlus (PLUS) was the largest market cap stock I've ever recommended. And, in part because of that, it was the stock I was certain was my "least risky" pick. Great management, strong growth in a strong industry, great operating metrics. And then... management decided to voluntarily de-list from NASDAQ!

Management had some repositioning and restructuring it wanted to do and didn't want the microscope associated with being fully reporting to impede them. Some institutional investors had to sell (their charters prohibited them from owning non-reporting stocks) and overall investor interest decreased dramatically, and so did volume and price. The stock fell and stayed well under my recommend price for years.

And now? 11 years later, PLUS trades at $89, which, even after all of the uncertainty and volatility, works out to be 45% annually. And that's if investors just bought at the time of my recommendation and held for 11 years.

However, the smart ones kept buying when the stock plummeted, as the underlying fundamentals remained strong and remained focused on relative value and didn't let the emotions of a stock moving down sway them from their course.

CASE STUDY: EXCELLIGENCE LEARNING CORPORATION

Formed in 2001, through the combination of Earlychildhood and SmarterKids.com, Excelligence Learning (LRNS, $5.44 up 0.10) is a developer, manufacturer and retailer of educational products for children from infancy to 12 years of age. The products are marketed to childcare programs, early childhood professionals, preschools, elementary schools, educators and parents.

The company has generated steady earnings growth (more than 16% after accounting for a $3 million income-tax benefit which is not normally part of net income) on healthy revenue growth, and has a very strong balance sheet. We expect this growth to continue over the long haul as a result of favorable demographic conditions and a sound business model. Currently, the stock is trading at just 18 times the company's trailing 12-months net income.

BUSINESS MODEL

One thing that stands out to us about Excelligence is its diverse and comprehensive business model. By not relying on any single business unit for revenue, the company has achieved record earnings. Products include an educational products catalog, the sale of early childhood furniture, a magazine published in print and online, and an innovative way of distributing school supplies through fund-raising programs. Not only does this model make good business sense, it also enables the company to address a broad spectrum of customer needs and realize substantial marketing and operating benefits.

First in Excelligence's organizational structure is Discount School Supply, a developer, manufacturer, importer, and vendor of 14 product lines, ranging from arts and crafts materials and school supplies, to educational toys, distributed through SmarterKids.com.

Second is Excelligence's online and catalog retailer of early childhood furniture and equipment, Marketing Logistics. Third, is an advertising-sponsored magazine for early childhood professionals, educators and parents called Earlychildhood NEWS. Finally, the company also creates custom apparel for schools' sports teams and fundraising efforts.

Further fueling or our endorsement of Excelligence is its distribution network. Typically, having a multi-disciplinary product line sold through multiple vendor types would present a logistical nightmare.

Excelligence is able to serve these two distinct markets with efficiency and effectiveness because it has warehouses across the U.S.; an order from the Discount School Supply catalog can be delivered within 48 hours to more than 90% of the U.S.

At this point, you might be noticing similarities between Excelligence and another of Bull Market MicroCap Review's favorite stocks, Collegiate Pacific (BOO, $8.35), another fast-growing institutional direct-selling company that distinguishes itself through great service and delivery on sales made through mail-order catalogs and fundraisers.

DEMOGRAPHIC TRENDS

While children's choices still get much of the credit for the ebb and flow -- and what is often perceived as fickleness -- in the educational product and toy market, the buck both starts and stops with the buyers of the items themselves. The future of the educational product market is bullish by virtue of the demographics of toy consumers. With the Baby Boomers aging, the grandparent population is quickly approaching a staggering 117 million by 2010.

This estimate, which represents a 34% increase over the number of eligible grandparents today, is expected to shape the market, with the educational value of products driving the entertainment value.

Why is this relevant? Because the boomers possess what is known in the toy and educational product industry as "waxing nostalgia." Parents who have recently become grandparents tend to shun the high-tech "educational" gadgets appreciated by today's Internet-savvy youth. Rather, they tend to purchase educational materials and toys that are reminiscent of their childhoods, and items that encourage educational and interpersonal involvement.

Going down the list of Excelligence Learning Company's magazines and online catalogues, the products for sale seek to both instill and capitalize on these virtues and many others. What's more, tutorial workshops are also increasing in number, as the Boomer generation wants to apply learning techniques that their parents and educators employed on them.

For a company that is specifically geared towards these educational products, the aging of America's population couldn't come at a better time.

FINANCIAL PERFORMANCE

Excelligence is just now beginning to enjoy the impact of the factors discussed above. They are likely to push the company to ever higher levels over and above its already strong financial performance. The Company had a 16% increase in EPS and a 10% growth in revenue through the first nine months of 2003.

The Early Childhood segment contributed $28.2 million in revenue and the Elementary School segment provided nearly $23 million for the quarter, a nice diversified balance.

We're particularly impressed that, in the face of ever-tightening school budgets and a recession hitting households, the company has been able to produce consistent gains. As the overall economy improves and education budgets begin to grow again, we would expect even better performance, generating $112 million in revenue (up 12% from 2002) and net income in the $3.5 million range ($0.38 fully diluted EPS) for the year.

FINANCIAL ANALYSIS

While the company's organizational and operating strategy has generated impressive financial performance, additional appeal as an investment can be gauged through ratio and financial analysis. Shares still hover in the $5 range, with only 7,000 shares or so trading on a daily basis. Though the company trades on the NASDAQ Small Cap Index, we believe that, based on its financial performance, earnings growth, and future prospects, Excelligence's shares are virtually unknown, and significantly undervalued.

To drive home this point, let's take a look at the price/book value ratio. In this analysis, we can effectively determine what premium the shares are trading at compared with the equity value (as derived from the company's balance sheet). More importantly in the case of Excelligence, we can see how this multiple compares with the rest of the industry.

The Company's tangible book value, or equity, remains just over $31 million, but its market cap is $50 million, fully diluted. Essentially, Excelligence's shares trade at 1.6x tangible book value, whereas the remainder of the educational products industry trades at a multiple closer to 7x book value.

We believe this significant gap will close over time, especially if its strong performance continues, and the company garners more attention, enabling its shares to move higher.

Next, we turn to a trusty valuation device, the PEG ratio. In this multiple, we divide Excelligence's P/E ratio by the earnings growth rate. Any number under 1.0 suggests that the company is undervalued. Based upon a P/E of 18 (low when compared with an industry average P/E of 50), and a current-year, real earnings growth rate of 40%, we have a PEG of 0.45! With continued strong financial performance and higher visibility among investors, Excelligence's shares will move up.

One note on comparative ratios: While the 7x book value and a 50 P/E seen in comparable stocks are high water marks to measure Excelligence's ratios against. But, the company has plenty of cash, a 2:1 current ratio, no long-term debt, and trades for barely 1.2 times book value (1.6 times tangible book), all of which makes for a solid foundation for future growth.

Trading at a P/E that is less than half of its growth rate makes for a solid foundation for the future growth of YOUR portfolio.

KEY FINANCIAL DATA

Ticker Symbol:	**LRNS**
Recent Price:	**$5.33**
52-Week High	**$7.40**
52-Week Low	**$1.99**
Market Cap	**$50M**
Forward PE	**14**
Forward PEG	**45**
Book Value Per Share	**$4.09**
Shares Outstanding	**9M**

Summary

Excelligence is yet another in a multitude of high quality companies whose shares trade at a substantial discount to its growth rate, almost entirely because no one knows the company's story. Institutions hold less than 3% of the shares outstanding.

This stock embodies the Bull Market MicroCap Reviews credo, "buy before the crowd." We've already seen what happens when the crowd comes in to our own Bull Market MicroCap Review's picks; both Collegiate Pacific (BOO, $8.35, down 0.15) and TVI Corp. (TVIN, $2.75, up 0.06) have seen large funds come into the stocks after readers accumulated significant positions at relatively low prices.

We would expect similar results here, OVER TIME. We've been fortunate with the timing of the crowd coming into the above-mentioned stocks. When the crowd will come, no one knows exactly. We can just be sure to own them before they move.

We believe Excelligence shares would be more fairly valued today up to the $9.00 range -- above even the 52-week high -- and we expect that the stock could reach the low teens over the next year or so.

EPILOGUE:

Not much to say about this one. Like DCAI, the macro picture in this space (education) was strong and superb management took full advantage. The company was acquired at 2.5x my recommended price within three years of my initial report.

CASE STUDY: HYPERCOM CORPORATION

KEY TAKEAWAYS:

Leading electronic payment solutions company poised to benefit from ongoing shift to debit, credit an stored value payments in the U.S. and around the world

Confluence of strategies brings HYC to a cash generation inflection point

Strategic acquisitions have provided substantial geographic and product diversification

Trades at just 2x cash

Recommendation: Buy rating with $4 price target, which equates to a discount to peers PAY and ING.PA

BUSINESS DESCRIPTION

Hypercom Corporation offers electronic payment solutions to financial institutions, payment processors, large retailers, and others. The company is one of the largest manufacturers of point-of-sale (POS) and network payment systems in the world and a truly global enterprise, with diversity geographically (71% of sales were international in '08) and in product/services mix (77%/23% in '08) that is unique among American competitors and has positioned the company to hold steady despite the current worldwide downturn and position it for further growth. The company also offers secure Web-enabled information and transaction terminals that work with its networking equipment and software applications for ecommerce, m-commerce, smart cards, and traditional payment applications, as well as consulting, system design and integration, and software development services in support of its core product offerings.

COMPETITIVE LANDSCAPE

The company faces competition from well-established companies with the main direct global competitors being Ingenico SA (ING.PA – Paris), a French company, and U.S.-based VeriFone Holdings, Inc. (PAY), both of which are publicly-held companies that are substantially larger and historically more profitable than the company. In any particular market, the company sometimes encounters nominal competition with local or regional providers.

In the company's multi-lane business line (department stores, grocery stores, quick serve restaurants, and discount merchants), it competes with additional vendors including Fujitsu, Hand Held Products (a division of Honeywell International Inc.) and Retail Solutions Inc.

COMPETITIVE STRATEGIES

Key elements of the company's competitive strategy to distinguish itself in the marketplace include the following in-progress initiatives:

Wireless Transactions. The company is committed to accommodating the growing demand for reliable, secure, convenient and cost-efficient wireless devices. Potential users of this technology include mobile merchants such as taxi and delivery drivers, in-flight airline service providers, stadium event operators, off-site services and pay-at-table restaurants.

These merchants are looking for a POS terminal that utilizes the convenience of wireless communication technologies and the security of being able to receive real-time authorizations with the reliability of a wired terminal. Simultaneously, the company is aggressively transitioning into the consumer transaction market by providing processing alternatives like stored value and prepaid replenishment services for the transportation sector and electronic wallet technology as an alternative to cash payments.

Emerging Geographic Regions. The company is committed to seeking opportunities to expand global market share by leveraging its product portfolio and distribution channels in emerging, high-growth regions in Europe, Asia-Pacific and South America.

In addition to expanding into new geographic markets, the company will benefit from a replacement cycle that is ongoing in various geographic regions for a variety of reasons, including valued-added technologies (signature capture, contactless, multi-application); new security standards (EMV and PCI); and newer communications technologies (wireless, IP connectivity).

Market-Driven Product Development. The company plans to focus its development efforts in highgrowth, customer-driven areas such as: enhanced security at the terminal and transaction level; advanced communications technologies such as IP-enabled and wireless terminals; multipleapplication; contactless technologies; and products for new vertical markets such as unattended/integrated kiosks (i.e. SmartPass for parking fees in DC).

Improve Total Cost Structure. To reduce the cost of manufacturing, in 2008 the company began a shift to contract manufacturing of most of its components and products, which has been almost totally completed as of this writing, which is resulting in reductions in cost of goods sold and G&A related to what had been in-house manufacturing.

As its current infrastructure is suitable to its current and foreseeable business requirements, the company should begin to see significant operating leverage allowing for higher volumes of revenue over existing G&A.

MAINTAINING A GROWTH POSTURE WHILE DIGESTING LARGE ACQUISITION

In April 2008, the company completed its acquisition of Thales eTransaction (TeT) for approximately $149.4 million in cash. TeT is a leading provider of secure card payment solutions in some of Europe's largest markets, including France, Germany, Spain and the United Kingdom. With the acquisition, Hypercom became one of the largest providers of electronic payment solutions and services in Western Europe, solidifying its position as the third largest provider globally.

Significantly, there is less than 1% overlap of customers between the two companies and a highly complimentary product line. Also meaningful is that the 2-year R&D cycle is estimated to fully integrate the two product platforms and should be complete within the next two quarters, at which point the company is likely to be able to converge and reduce previous annual R&D expenses. Redundant sales expense should have also been reduced by that time.

Although its acquisition and subsequent integration of TeT has required and will continue to require significant effort on its part and will be a major focus throughout most of the remainder of 2009, the company could take advantage of the current weak economic climate to augment its growth by acquiring complementary businesses, new products to enhance its core competencies, or new technologies to complement its research and development activities. The company may be somewhat constrained in this by its limited liquid assets, which stand at a little over $30mm.

INNOVATION, LEADERSHIP IN NEW MARKETS DRIVE GROWTH

The company announced last week that its worldwide initiative for high security electronic health card systems is accelerating. The company's medMobile™ terminal, its fourth healthcare device released in support of Germany's e-Health card program was recently made the first and only such solution approved by the German health care organization Gematik, which is also providing reimbursement to healthcare buyers who purchase the device.

The roll-out of the product commenced in December 2008 when the first unit was installed at a medical practice during a ceremony attended by representatives of the German government, health insurance companies and the medical practitioners' self-governing body. medMobile is a secure mobile device specifically designed to support the thousands of physicians who make house calls/visits throughout Germany and those that practice at hospitals, pharmacies and geriatric institutions, such as residential care homes.

Hypercom is the only transaction solutions provider with a complete family of approved high security data transaction products for Germany's e-Health card program, which is one of the largest e-Health IT projects worldwide with a planned deployment of more than 80 million electronic health insurance cards.

Hypercom's solutions to facilitate electronic health care also have a foothold in a number of other countries including Australia, France, the United States and elsewhere.

The e-Health business currently accounts for virtually none of the company's revenues but has the potential to become a significant growth driver for the company as early as 2010, the prospects of which it appears have yet to be included in analyst estimates.

2008 REVIEW AND OUTLOOK

Net revenue for 2008 was $437.3 million, a 51.0% increase over the twelve months ended December 31, 2007, with much of the increase ($120 million, or 41%) due to its acquisition of TeT.

The company realized almost 10% growth separate of the TeT acquisition and attributes much of this growth to a strong increase in demand for its countertop and multilane products in the U.S.

Product gross profit was 31.6% in 2008, up from 27.7% in 2007, principally due to the result of higher gross margin on TeT product sales, changes in product mix for countertop, mobile, and multilane products, as well as efficiencies gained from transitioning to contract manufacturing, a process begun during the first half of 2008, but which results were not fully felt for the whole year 2008.

Margins on services declined almost 10% from 27% to 17% in 2007 and 2008, respectively, primarily due to competitive pressures and one-time expenses (such as severance payments) in major services market, Brazil. While service margins are expected to remain weak for the near future, offsetting efforts such as the introduction of a higher-margin product in Brazil are well underway.

COMPARABLES

The largest direct competitors to HYC in North America is VeriFone Holdings, Inc., (PAY) which offers technology and services as solutions for electronic payment transaction handling and Ingenico, S.A. (ING.PA – Paris). Like HYC, both companies offer products, related services and serve similar customers such as global financial institutions, payment processors, government organizations, and retailers. This is where the similarities end.

PAY, despite having just this quarter returned barely to cash flow positive (1.5% cash flow margin over last two quarters vs. 2.5% for HYC), dramatically eroding equity (105% reduction – currently in the negative) – vs. 50% reduction for HYC) and substantial debt (60% of sales vs. barely 10% for HYC) trades at an enterprise value (EV) to sales ratio of 1.18 vs. 0.21 for HYC, which would suggest an 80% discount on that basis. Price to sales is little better in parity with PAY priced at 77% of sales vs. 19% of sales for HYC, an implied discount of 75%.

ING.PA is an excellent comp for a variety of reasons. HYC's geographic footprint is almost identical, with just a slightly higher mix of Northern Europe revenues (25% vs. 18%) – the remaining geographies are within 5%. Both companies saw Q1

'09 revenue decline about 22%; both had slight organic growth from '07 to '08 (HYC's 10% to ING.PA's 5%). Yet ING.PA trades at 1.27x revenue vs. 0.21x for HYC.

Why? Net income. ING.PA has had it the last two years, HYC has not. Here is where I think a key trend line in HYC bears pointing out vis-à-vis ING.PA. ING.PA had a history of minimal cash flow until hitting "critical mass" in 2005 when revenues reached about $500mm in sales – very near to where HYC is, after which ING.PA started printing cash - $16mm in 2006, $45mm in 2007and $55mm in 2008.

With the company's significant expansion into Europe, its market leadership in the e-health greenfield that could represent billions of dollars worldwide, its gains in operating efficiencies post-TeT merger and from its move to contract manufacturing, leads us to believe HYC is at an inflection point at which it should begin to throw off significant amounts of cash within several quarters, yielding tremendous upside.

SHORT TERM BUY WITH UPSIDE

In the near term, the stock is priced at a discount and represents a short-term trade. VeriFone (PAY) trades at a price of 77% of sales vs. 16% of sales for HYC despite 1) growing more slowly 2) similar gross margins but only 75% of SG&A 3) substantially more relative debt (60% of sales) 4) substantially negative net worth 5) similar cyclical losses and write downs. Every single insider transaction since January 2008 has been a purchase – no sales – at prices as high as $3.86/shares (so have most of the PAY insider transactions, which would tend to be a leading indicator and show confidence and strength in the space).

An argument can be made that HYC could run 300% higher to the mid $4s and still trade only in parity with the market leader in the space, and more on parity with Ingenico (ING.PA) (5x up from current price, or $7) as the company begins to generate cash flow, but I would expect this to take through the better part of 2010. Even at a modest discount of 20-25% still offers tremendous upside in NYC shares from current levels.

RISKS

Large competitors with greater resources than company

Prolonged economic slowdown

Greater than anticipated costs and/or time to integrate TeT acquisition

Technological obsolescence

COMPANIES MENTIONED

VeriFone Holdings, Inc. (PAY)

Ingenico, S.A. (ING.PA)

EPILOGUE:

It's not too often I find an "under-the-radar" microcap trading on the New York Stock Exchange. Hypercom was an amazing opportunity that was acquired within 18 months of my initial report at almost 6x my recommend price.

CASE STUDY: LIFE PARTNERS HOLDINGS

LIFE PARTNERS HOLDINGS (LPHI, $6.84, up 0.05) is the largest, oldest, and fastest growing life settlement company in the United States. A life settlement company facilitates the purchase of life insurance policies from older individuals and the terminally ill in order to place cash in the hands of the policyholders.

Life Partners has been in business since 1991 and has completed over 4,000 transactions with a face value of nearly a quarter of a billion dollars. Life Partners is the only life settlement company listed on Nasdaq.

The company's revenues have grown an average of 67% a year over the past three years. That's 67% during the worst economic times in over a decade. This indicates that, as you might expect with a company whose business is focused on something as steady as life expectancy, the company's business model is recession resistant.

For the nine months ending November 2003, Life Partners recorded net income of $1.7 million, representing a 53% increase from the same nine months a year earlier. Return on equity was 59%.

COMPANY BACKGROUND

Headquartered in Waco, Texas, Life Partners Holdings is the parent company of two subsidiaries, Life Partners and Extended Life Services. Life Partners has been in operation since 1991 and provides viatical settlement services to assist terminally ill individuals in facilitating the purchase of life insurance policies, at a discount. Acquired in 2000, Extended Life Services provides senior life settlement services to assist older individuals, who aren't terminally ill, by facilitating the purchase of life insurance policies.

Clients of Life Partners use the money received from the sale for a variety of things, including paying for medical expenses or personal debt, and taking a dream vacation in their last days. Extended Life clients typically use the proceeds to help fund retirement, make a major purchase, or give the money to family or charities. Historically, Life Partners has provided the majority of revenues for the company, primarily from clients living with AIDS. The senior life settlement business is relatively new, but it has a lot of potential because of the aging of the population. Importantly, baby boomers are just now entering their 60's. Life Partners is considered an innovator and the pioneer of the life settlement purchase process, and, as such, we expect the company to gain first mover advantage in any coming developments within the industry.

FINANCIALS

Life Partners sits near the top of the Financial Services industry in most metrics of financial performance. The overall industry yields a 36% return on equity -- Life Partners has generated 59%. In the nine months through November 30th, 2003, revenue and earnings per share jumped 30% and 50%, respectively, placing it among the best performing Financial Services companies in the country. A 15% net profit margin also places it among the most profitable in the industry. It has a strong balance sheet with a debt to equity ratio of a 0.12 and over $5 million in cash and marketable securities, providing for adequate coverage of near-term working capital needs.

MANAGEMENT COMMITMENT TO SHAREHOLDER VALUE

In analyzing the actions of the management team, it's clear that extra steps have been taken to maximize shareholder value. Three times in the past three years, the company announced a stock buyback of over 250,000 shares. These were initiated to get undervalued stock off the market and boost the per share value of the remaining shares. Management alone owns 59% of the outstanding common shares, so their own personal fortunes are closely tied to the well being of the stock. Finally, the company is listed on two stock exchanges, the Nasdaq in the United States and the Berlin Stock Exchange in Europe, providing the company international exposure and higher levels of future sponsorship and liquidity.

A dividend also bolsters shareholder value. In 2003, the company paid a dividend of $0.12 per share, generating a yield of 1.8%. We expect that management would increase the dividend as earnings allow. With the new dividend tax structure passed last year by Congress, dividend income is now an even more attractive means by which to return value to shareholders.

GROWTH PROSPECTS

The company is a strong performer, managed by a team of shareholder-centric professionals. But what about the industry in which it operates? This industry, especially life settlement, is ready to explode. The dynamics of the economies and populations here and around the world provide the right mix of revenue opportunity for both the near term and the long term.

SKYROCKETING MEDICAL COSTS

In the U.S., the cost of medical insurance is reaching all-time highs. As a result, many people now need to divert resources from other areas of spending to cover this increase. In 2004, medical insurance premiums, copays, and deductibles will rise an average of 40% for consumers. For the terminally ill and elderly, who spend 11% of their total income on healthcare and typically live on a fixed income from social security or a retirement account, this adjustment will not be easy. As a result, they will need to find alternative means to cover rising costs. We believe that life settlement is a viable and in some cases necessary alternative.

THE BABY-BOOMERS

For five decades, the baby boomer generation has been a freight train loaded with market opportunities, and its next stop might just well be at the doorstep of the life settlement industry. In 2003, the baby boomer population was 78 million. With spending power of $2.1 trillion a year, 10% of which is spent on insurance products, this demographic represents a powerful and highly potent future for Life Partners. Furthermore, the life expectancy of the average American is increasing, which means additional sources of income and/or capital will be needed to fund more lengthy retirements. Since 1980, life expectancy in the U.S. has risen 5%, to 79.5 for females and 74.1 for males. In 2000, there were 35 million people over the age of 65. By 2030, that number is expected to be 70 million. Recent estimates have valued the life settlement market at $135 billion. You can imagine how much the market could grow in the next 5-10 years.

INTERNATIONAL EXPANSION

As for growth in the international market, the company is adding to its existing base of international business with an eye toward China. The market for life insurance in China is sizable and has grown 35x over the past decade, with most of the market still untapped or underserved. In the year 2000, the total face value of Chinese life insurance policies was $14 billion (compared to about $1 trillion overall), representing a $13.6 billion increase in value since 1989. With the population of elderly Chinese growing rapidly over the next 25 years, China provides a virtual "green field" for a thriving life settlement industry.

While life settlements have yet to pick up much of a following in China, it's probably just a matter of time before their benefits are recognized. When they are, Life Partners should be well positioned to capitalize. The country's financial markets are maturing and are set to have a strong 2004. As a result, overall financial savvy is expected to increase rapidly and provide a foundation for the broad acceptance of life settlements as a financial option to the elderly.

The company has international experience, with 55% of their 2003 revenue coming from overseas clients. In addition, the company already has a business presence in the Far East. Relationships in this part of the world are vitally important for success -- and are some of the more difficult to build -- because of cultural differences. As such, Life Partners has a competitive advantage over current and future players in the industry that will be hard to catch up to.

KEY FINANCIAL DATA

Ticker Symbol:	**LPHI**
Recent Price:	**$6.84**
52-week high:	**$7.50**
52-week low:	**$2.40**
Market Cap:	**$62M**
P/E:	**26**
P/Sales:	**8.5**
Dividend:	**$0.12**
Yield:	**1.8%**
Fiscal Year End:	**2/28**
Shares Outstanding:	**9,711,400**
Insider Ownership:	**59%**
Employees:	**32**

ANALYSIS AND SUMMARY

We expect another strong year for the company, with revenues forecast to top $17 million, up about 40%, and EPS of 29-31 cents, up 50%, from a year ago. Currently, the stock is priced at $6.84 per share, or roughly 26 times trailing 12-month earnings, with a forward PEG of 0.5. We are looking for the PEG to move toward 1.0 over the next few quarters, putting the stock in the $12 range. That makes it a good value up to the $9 range.

Life Partners is a leader in a cutting-edge industry. Management has proven it knows how to produce shareholder value in a fast-paced environment; and the overall industry is poised for growth both now and 15-20 years into the future. We're going to watch this one carefully. It's the kind of stock that could become a "core" MicroCap holding for many years to come.

EPILOGUE:

Life Partners Holdings (LPHI) is another stock my investors made a lot of money on, which later succumbed to a tightened regulatory environment in their space and management hubris (they didn't appear to believe the new rules applied to them).

The stock went from my $3.71 recommend price (trading mere thousands of shares a day) to $26.00 (trading hundreds of thousands of shares). Then, within a few years, they filed bankruptcy. Even so, following my investing rules at the time of the recommendation and for a long time thereafter, investors made money and were out before the worst came.

CASE STUDY: MATRIXX INITIATIVES

The first company we bring to our MicroCap Review subscribers for 2004 is Matrixx Initiatives (MTXX, $18.05, down 0.10). Though this Phoenix-based company is on the large side as far as MicroCaps go, we believe it to be a "rapid riser."

As a matter of fact, we happen to know quite a bit about the company. Your Editor, Steve Kann, actually participated in the company's initial public offering in 1996, while working in the underwriter's Manhattan office.

Although the company has gone through much restructuring and repositioning over the years, it is now poised for excellent performance over the next few years. Matrixx develops, produces and sells over-the-counter (OTC) pharmaceutical products, particularly cold remedy products with an emphasis on those that utilize unique delivery systems.

We believe that the company is approaching a critical juncture where its popularity, profitability and stock will continue to move.

There has been strong momentum in the stock recently, sending it beyond our coverage. This is why we are bringing it to your attention now while it's still under-followed and within our coverage parameters.

There's one huge reason we think this stock will continue to be a big winner: It's cornerstone product, a product that Editor Steve and his family unequivocally swear by has had a profound impact on the quality of their health. In fact, through evangelical referrals to others, Steve figures that he has been responsible for a tiny fraction of Matrixx's yearly sales growth!

REDEFINING A PRODUCT CATEGORY

As it stands, Matrixx has commenced what will prove to be a major growth period. Following the company's restructuring (detailed below), their subsidiary, Zicam, has been busy producing, marketing and selling several different products under the Zicam brand geared to reducing the severity and duration of the common cold. Independent studies have confirmed that patients using Zicam Cold Remedy enjoy a 74% reduction in the duration and severity of cold symptoms.

Product: Zicam Cold Remedy Nasal Gel
Description: Reduces severity and duration of common cold

Product: Zicam Cold Remedy Swabs adult size
Description: Nasal Swab cold remedy

Product: Zicam Cold Remedy Swabs for kids
Description: Nasal Swab cold remedy

Product: Zicam Allergy Relief
Description: Homeopathic Nasal Gel to control allergy symptoms

Product: Zicam Extreme Congestion Relief
Description: Nasal Gel to relieve nasal congestion

Product: Zicam Sinus Relief
Description: Nasal Gel which enhances benefits of "Extreme Congestion Relief"

Product: Zicam Nasal Moisturizer
Description: Non Medicated nasal moisturizer

Clearly, the Zicam products are targeted to the cough and cold market. But, one would likely ask, isn't this market saturated?

The answer is both yes and no. The retail cold market is estimated at more than $3 billion annually through a wide variety of tablets, liquids, nasal sprays and syrups that provide relief and remedy to cold and sinus congestion sufferers. There are plenty of brands that attempt to remedy the 1 billion common colds that occur each year with OTC pills and syrups.

However, while the Tylenol Colds and Nyquils of the pharmaceutical world help to eliminate the symptoms of colds, these same symptoms force 100 million Americans to take days off work or school each year to recuperate. Therefore, a company that could handle the same load of symptoms, but work faster to eliminate them, would inevitably be in demand. Thus, a main source of our enthusiasm for Matrixx comes by virtue of the extremely high efficacy of its products, and its specialty in alternative delivery systems that are much less invasive and work faster than their pill/liquid counterparts.

What's more, product sales have just about achieved critical mass. (This is the point at which many consumer products achieve sufficient sales volume, breadth of distribution, and brand awareness as to gain geometric sales growth versus what might have been earlier linear sales growth.)

COMPETITIVE ADVANTAGE

Matrixx has built a competitive advantage through its experience in producing, developing, and selling alternative pharmaceutical delivery systems. The company started as Gum Tech International in 1991, at which time it developed, manufactured, and sold nutritional and healthcare related chewing gum products -- the chewing gum at that time being the alternative delivery system of choice for the company's products.

The company exited the chewing gum business after it acquired all of Gel Tech in 2001. It reincorporated as Matrixx and began producing faster-working homeopathic nasal gel products based on a proprietary zincum gluconicum delivery system.

Now, Zicam's homoeopathic nasal gel Cold Remedy and Swabs, which are based on the zincum gluconicum delivery system, account for more than 70% of the company's sales. What's powering such prominence?

For starters, management has dedicated itself to increasing the company's marketing and sales efforts. Such efforts include improving the timing and consistency of marketing activities compared to previous years, executing effective trial generating programs, implementing programs with retailers to enhance consumer awareness of Matrixx's products, and more importantly, gaining increased recommendations from healthcare professionals.

To the welcome ears of management and shareholders, Matrixx's greatest promoter, in fact, has come from the medical and journalistic community.

EXTERNAL PRAISE

In October 2000, Ear, Nose & Throat Journal showed that Zicam Cold Remedy reduced the duration of the common cold when taken at the onset of symptoms. What's more, in the January 2003 issue of QJM: An International Journal of Medicine, zincum gluconicum nasal gel (Zicam Cold Remedy) was shown to reduce the duration and symptoms of the common cold when treatment was started as late as the second day.

Of particular significance to Matrixx's competitors, a USA Today article revealed that Zicam's new zinc nasal spray knocked out the common cold in a day and a half in the first scientific test of the product, while cold symptoms lingered for about nine days in placebo users. With testimonials like these, it's no surprise that demand for Zicam not long ago surpassed supply (a backlog that has since been satisfied through management's decision to switch suppliers).

A side note: Editor Steve Kann has been buying Zicam products continuously for several years and has made a habit of informally monitoring shelf space and availability of the products. In the two supermarkets where he regularly shops, shelf space for all

Zicam products has tripled in the last year, and, for the first time ever, the product was completely sold out two different times over the last 30 days, an anecdotal sign that demand continues to accelerate.

BUSINESS OVERVIEW

Matrixx sells to pharmacies such as CVS and retail stores like Wal-Mart (10 customers accounted for more than 70% of total sales in 2002). Since its introduction in 1999, sales of Zicam Cold Remedy have grown steadily. Fueling this growth is augmented customer awareness, spurred by marketing and public relations efforts, and word-of-mouth experience by consumers.

What's more, as a delivery system innovator, Matrixx has reached an entirely different demographic than its competitors by creating alternative delivery systems for cold and allergy remedies. Not only does the company differ from the standard pill market with its various nasal spray-based remedies, but in response to customer feedback it also caters to the market of consumers who dislike nasal sprays.

Zicam Cold Remedy Swabs and Zicam Cold Remedy Swabs-Kids Size, which contain the same ingredients as Zicam Cold Remedy, have enjoyed sales almost equal to their long-established brethren on store shelves, making this a very attractive growth sector for the company going forward.

FINANCIAL PERFORMANCE

Though product sales are growing rapidly, this may just be the tip of the iceberg. In many companies similar to Matrixx, hefty research, development, marketing, and sales costs that potentially eat away at profits have most investors ready to accept losses for a reasonable period of time.

What strikes us about Matrixx, however, is the company's lean cost structure, which has created strong and growing profitability, with higher levels yet likely to be achieved, as outlined below.

There have been a lot of tax-related adjustments made to its financials over the last few quarters, in part due to the aforementioned restructuring. We're going to make every effort to compare apples to apples by focusing on income before accounting for any adjustments -- the adjustments appear to be over. Nonetheless, the company does have substantial tax advantages due to past losses, that will have the effect of producing more cash than our net income projections here will indicate.

Over the last 12 months, Matrixx has earned about $2.5 million -- in absolute, after-tax terms -- on nearly $37 million in revenues. In Q303, the company shipped three new Zicam Cold Remedy products: Oral Mist, Chewables, and RapidMelts. These immediately impacted sales figures. For 3Q03, sales increased to $13.4 million, or 160% higher than 3Q02.

Over this time R&D and overhead increased only 42%. On a net income basis -- again in absolute terms -- Matrix earned 245% more than it had a year earlier. Compare these figures with an industry average growth of 3.6% last quarter and Matrixx's performance rightfully stands out.

As the company continues in its effort to capitalize on its nasal gel technology; to develop new products and delivery systems; and to market those products, we expect sales/earnings figures to continue to increase markedly. Management has stated that sales for 2003 are expected to be "at least" 50% greater than the $23 million reported in 2002, and that EPS should come in at around $0.30 per share. It is our opinion that the company will soundly beat this estimate, and, in fact, we wouldn't be surprised if EPS were closer to $0.40.

Matrixx's business model is one of efficiency and effectiveness. Currently, Matrixx's only office in Phoenix employs 14 people. While the company outsources some of its swab manufacturing, Matrixx maintains in-house R&D and sales and marketing departments. By combining these operations under one roof, the company earns $200,000 per employee on almost $3 million in revenue. We don't know that we've ever seen revenue/income per employee this high in a company before.

We expect management to keep a tight rein on expenses while leveraging its existing and expanding distribution network to grow sales. Hear this: Over the past three years the company's revenues have grown from $13 million to $16 million to $24 million to $37 million. Over the same period, overhead (selling, general and administrative expenses) has come in at $17 million, $17 million, $15.5 million, $17 million -- flat expenses and almost TRIPLE the revenue!

This is the classic outsource model. Core overhead and R&D remained fixed while distribution, sales, and gross profit expanded, creating sustainable growth in operating and net income margins. As such, we see 50% per year growth in revenue, with net income posting triple-digit gains for the next few years.

And we believe that the overall Zicam product line has real homerun potential, the kind that made Cold-eez (not the product Zicam is) an international consumer product freight train. It's exactly the type of product that can see extraordinary revenue spikes as word-of-mouth and broadcast media coverage increase.

KEY FINANCIAL DATA

Ticker Symbol:	**MTXX**
Recent Price:	**$18.02**
52 Week High:	**$18.52**
52-Week Low:	**$6.21**
Market Cap:	**$170 million**
PE:	**60**
PEG	**0.27**
Book Value/Share	**3.96**
Shares Outstanding:	**9.4 Million**

PRICE/VALUE ANALYSIS

The institutional investor community has just begun to notice the company, which partly accounts for the recent rise. Don't let this put you off -- it's still early in the process and momentum is a powerful thing.

Unlike the vast majority of MicroCap stocks, which most institutions tend to stay away from, 10% of Matrixx's shares are currently institutionally owned. 10% is the top end of our parameters for institutional ownership. Any more and we wouldn't consider Matrixx an undiscovered stock.

What's more, these institutions comprise a who's-who of the institutional market, with Merrill Lynch, US Bancorp Asset Management, Oberweis Asset Management, Barclays Global Investors International, and Dimensional Fund Advisors accounting for significant ownership.

The company has a market capitalization of nearly $170 million and a PE of 60, based on 30 cents. We see EPS closer to $0.40, which would make the current PE 45. Still, we consider shares to be attractively priced relative to the recent and expected earnings growth rate of over 100% over the coming year.

On a PEG (price to earnings growth) basis, earnings growth translates to a PEG of 0.6 - quite low. We believe that Matrixx's PEG will trade much closer to our ideal of 1.0, meaning a range of up to $30 over the next year or two.

SUMMARY

Matrixx is on autopilot, with distribution established, R&D budgets fixed, new product offerings planned, and very bright prospects ahead. We're catching the company at the exact moment when it has created the most operational leverage -- the point at which earnings growth can far outpace revenue growth.

That's saying something for a company growing revenue at more than 50% per year.

We believe that with the addition of several new products to pump into the company's large and growing distribution pipeline, rapid word of mouth, and an enhanced marketing/brand awareness campaign in the offing, the company may well exceed management's bold guidance for the coming quarters.

We're telling you plainly, if your throat starts to scratch or you feel a hint of sniffles, get yourself right to the store and try these products! You'll feel better -- we promise! And if you start accumulating shares of Matrixx today, at prices up to $22 or so, your portfolio should be feeling a lot better this time next year!

EPILOGUE:

Another incredibly up-and-down ride. When I first looked at Matrixx, it had a great, proprietary product (that I used myself and knew to be effective), awesome growth and a huge market left to address.

Not too long after my recommendation the company was sued, and the stock took a huge hit. The suits when on for years and stock languished. About six years after my initial report the company was acquired at a price about half of where I recommended it, making it one of my worst performing picks. The company's products are still going strong today.

CASE STUDY: RMS TITANIC

We always go deep to find great stocks for you. This time we went really deep -- in fact, 2 1/2 miles deep. RMS TITANIC (SOST, $2.00) is the only company permitted by law to recover objects from the wreck of the Titanic. The company was granted salvor-in-possession rights to the wreck by a United States Federal Court. The company conducted six research and recovery expeditions to the Titanic, and recovered 6,000 artifacts, which represent less than 5% of the artifacts available for recovery. The company continues to maintain its salvor-in-possession status by making periodic expeditions to the shipwreck. The company is now directly engaged in the business of exhibiting the artifacts recovered from the Titanic, and owns five touring museum exhibits of the artifacts it salvaged from the ship.

While embroiled in the legal tangle over rights to these artifacts, the company made the decision to license the rights to media giant, Clear Channel, through its Clear Channel Exhibitions subsidiary. The tours have been wildly successful over the last five years, attracting millions of visitors in countries ranging from Switzerland to Argentina to Japan. After the courts recently ruled in the company's favor on its rights to the artifacts, it canceled the Clear Channel deal earlier this month and began to stage the exhibits itself. Hundreds of museums worldwide have wished to have the exhibits for their own communities, but have not yet had the opportunity. Already, dozens of venues worldwide have requested the exhibit, enough to keep the current collection of artifacts touring for the next five years.

BUILDING BLOCKS

The company's legal victory and the popularity of the Titanic artifacts built a launch for the RMS Titanic to become a full-blown exhibition company. It will take advantage of favorable demographic trends, the growth of alternative entertainment, and in its own fortunate position of having one of the marquee core assets of any such company in the world, to conduct other non-Titanic exhibitions.

To this end, management has hired key personnel -- former Clear Channel executives who managed the Titanic exhibits while under the previous arrangement -- to administer and manage the design, marketing, and administration of current and future exhibitions. The company is well on its way to fully implementing this business plan, having announced both the staging of Titanic exhibits in three cities beginning in May, and the development of a new and separate museum or alternative venue exhibition that it expects to announce in the summer.

FINANCIALS

Two factors point toward this being a tremendous investment opportunity. First, for years the company had been burdened by the legal costs of defending its claim on the artifacts, costs that have now all but disappeared. Second, simple math and an analysis of the prior Clear Channel licensing deal allow us to extrapolate to estimate the financial results of the company touring the exhibits itself.

By virtue of the royalty Clear Channel paid to RMS Titanic in the last two years, as reported in the company's filings, Clear Channel had to have generated approximately $13 million in revenue from touring the exhibits in each of the last two years, which generated approximately $2.6 million for the company in each year. Our sources in the exhibition industry tell us that, based on the numbers generated by Clear Channel on the Titanic exhibits, it would be reasonable to assume that Clear Channel realized a profit of around $5 million each year, before accounting for the royalty. That's a profit that RMS Titanic can now generate for itself.

Significantly, the Clear Channel tours utilized only three exhibits. This limited both run times and potential venues. By contrast, RMS Titanic has five exhibits ready to tour, all built at Clear Channel's expense, providing an opportunity to generate more revenue than Clear Channel possibly could have.

Let's stick to just the known revenue for now, even while keeping in mind the upside. The company has little overhead outside of its staging of the exhibits and, as such, stands to cut into that $5 million profit very little.

Furthermore, with a fairly large net loss carry forward, the company won't be paying tax for a while, making the $5 million pure income. With 19 million shares outstanding, annual EPS would be around $0.26, making the forward PE at the current price under 5.

A company press release earlier this week backs this up with EPS estimates of 10-14 cents for fiscal year 2005 ending February 28th, 2005. Since the exhibits are planned for roll out in May and June, this allows for only about eight months of touring in the current fiscal year.

On an annualized basis, the company's estimates hit 15-20 cents, near our own expectations. Our guess is that management is hedging on estimates to account for potentially longer lead times getting the exhibits deployed, and costs associated with bringing online other touring assets the company has stated it intends to deploy in the current fiscal year.

However, let's see what the baseline company will look like a year from now, with all five exhibits deployed and a new non-Titanic exhibit gaining hold. Clear Channel generated average revenue of $4.3 million per exhibit, so it would be reasonable to assume that RMS would generate over $20 million annually from all five exhibits, which would likely add about $3.5 million to operating income, taking it to $8 million. We don't know much about the non-Titanic exhibit so we won't even include it here, although it is likely to provide at least another $1 million in operating income (or else management wouldn't undertake it in the first place).

However, even at $8 million operating income as a baseline for FY 2006, the company would begin to pay some taxes, but not much, so we estimate net income will be close to $7 million. Assuming that shares outstanding grow to around 20 million, which is likely to happen through small financings or stock option plans for employees, EPS would come in around 35 cents, which represents 100% YoY growth. Considering the stock trades at only 9x annualized EPS, the PEG is under 0.10!

Here's one more wrinkle: A happy byproduct of the recent court proceedings is that the artifacts were required to be appraised by a third party. Court records indicate that the assets have been appraised at $75 million. The stock's current market cap is $37 million, less than half that.

KEY FINANCIAL DATA

Ticker Symbol:	**SOST**
Recent Price:	**$2.00**
52-week High:	**$2.30**
52-week Low:	**$0.06**
Market Cap:	**$37 million**
Current P/E:	**99**
Fiscal Year:	**2/28**
Shares Outstanding:	**19 million**
Insider Ownership:	**19%**

THE BOTTOM LINE

RMS Titanic is the sole custodian of a dramatic piece of human history. For a century, people from all over the world have been drawn to the tragic story. Most have read about it in books or seen the blockbuster Hollywood spectacles. RMS Titanic now provides citizens of the world an opportunity to get up close and personal with the story, and put themselves in the presence of both souls who went down with the ship and pieces of the mighty ship itself. They've been coming in droves.

These are the kinds of investments we love: Finding a story one has to dig to uncover -- it doesn't just show up on bulletin boards or in junk mail -- and finding a business at a dramatic inflection point. The stock trades nicely. It is priced at a fraction of its baseline earnings and implied growth rate. As of yet, it has little or no institutional following, just the way we like it; investors who move in now will be early and beat the crowd.

We anticipate continued strong operating results for at least the next six quarters. Based on the consistent success of the Titanic exhibits in the past; the company's ability to stage two additional Titanic exhibits, and the overwhelming demand for the exhibits worldwide, the stock warrants a forward PE of 40. On the current baseline annualized EPS, a PE of 40 puts the stock at $7, and a PE of 40 on the implied EPS derived from the additional Titanic exhibits and one non-Titanic exhibit, will put the stock in double digits over the next two years.

At this time, we would accumulate the stock up to the $4 range, with possible adjustments upward in the coming months, as details and impending developments emerge.

EPILOGUE:

RMS Titanic (SOST), later Premier Exhibitions (PRXI). Yes, it seems like tempting fate when you recommend an investment related to the greatest shipwreck in world history, but the story was really compelling and remains so today. What's instructive about this experience more so than any of my other picks (although they're illustrative of this point also) is that, when I found the stock, it was trading just a few thousand shares a day at $0.95 (although I didn't complete my due diligence and write up the stock until it was trading at $2.00).

Imagine, just a few thousand dollars a day were trading hands in this stock at under $1.00. Within three years, the stock was trading hundreds of thousands of shares a day at $15 (it traded as high as $17.60, but I recommended selling at $9.00).

This was classic information arbitrage. You could not dig into this story in 2004 and not see a stock that should be trading much higher . . . but no one was watching! This didn't mean that the company's fundamentals weren't strong and improving or that the stock wasn't ridiculously undervalued; it just meant that not a sufficient number of people knew enough about the company for the market to properly price the story. As such, no one was buying at $0.95 but investors couldn't get enough of it at $15.00.

Years later there would be a management change and missteps, and now the company is about to be delisted, trading at just $0.11. So, again, we stick to our knitting, buying the stock at a discount to value, watching to make sure that value continues to exceed price until our target price is met, and then we unemotionally and in a disciplined way move out of the position, take profits and look for another opportunity.

CASE STUDY: SPORT SUPPLY GROUP, INC.

KEY TAKEAWAYS:

Business model has counter-recessionary characteristics; budget squeezes turn institutional customers away from convenience (retail) toward value (mail order/generic) buying

Opportunity from being painted inaccurately with "consumer discretionary" brush

Continued operational improvement despite economic downturn;

Trading at a relative discount (31%, 33% and 50%) to three closest comparables on several bases despite RBI's higher growth rates and consistency

Significant operational leverage; $7mm increase in gross profit dropped directly to '08 bottom line

Recommendation: Buy rating with a $11 price target, which equates to 0.5x 2009 revenue and 12x

2009 EPS vs. EPS growth of 18% in 2009 vs. 2008

BUSINESS DESCRIPTION

Sport Supply Group, Inc. (www.sportsupply.com), markets 22,000 products through its three million catalogues mailed annually to over 200,000 customers and prospects, making it the largest (by 5x) factory-direct manufacturer and mail-order distributor of sporting goods and equipment to the institutional market (schools, churches, government agencies, etc.) in the United States. Its fourpronged marketing capability (catalogs, 100+ outside sales professionals, e-commerce and inside telemarketing), which brings the company into direct contact with customers across multiple platforms, is a major differentiating element of the company's business and absolutely unique in the space.

The business model has proven to be counter-recessionary over the last 37 years since the customer spends from a government budget and in tough economic times stretches to make the same budget go further or maintain services at a reduced budget by switching away from products priced at retail at the local sporting goods store to the company's factory-direct (discounted) pricing (10-30% off local options).

ALL-STAR MANAGEMENT

Before Founder and former CEO Michael Blumenfeld started what was then Collegiate Pacific (RBI) in 1998, in his first 25 years in the industry, he had successfully built from the ground up two other sporting goods companies that sold exclusively to institutional customers, an industry niche that he essentially created: BSN in 1972 and the original Sport Supply Group in 1991, both of which were built to about $100 million and then sold (Sport Supply was subsequently acquired by RBI in 2006 and the name adopted).

Mike's son, Adam, RBI's current CEO, grew up in the business, has been with the various companies for 16 years, and carries on his father's impressive operating legacy. The core of RBI's management team and employee base has remained largely intact through the multiple iterations and represent hundreds of years of combined experience in the sporting goods and equipment industry. This management team has never had a down year in revenue in 38 years (see the chart of RBI's revenue and cash flow growth since 2004 below under "Strong Operating Results"); and while revenue may be flat to down during the rest of the current, unprecedented downturn, cash flow should continue to accelerate.

Utilizing what the Blumenfelds call their "greatest hits" culled from their first two successful runs in the business, RBI has already become larger in scale than the first two companies and still has plenty of upside – even as the largest company in the country serving the $4 billion institutional sporting goods/ equipment market ($6 billion including team apparel), the company's market share at $250 million is barely 4%, leaving plenty of "green field" for organic growth and targeted strategic acquisitions.

PROPRIETARY PRODUCTS AND DISTRIBUTION

RBI's one-stop shop for a customer's needs differentiates the company in a fragmented and noisy field. Whereas potential competitors either only distribute, or have minimal manufacturing capabilities, RBI not only maintains an enormous marketing and distribution capacity but is also an ambitious manufacturer of its own proprietary and direct-import products – what they call "bent metal" (bleachers, balls, weight lifting equipment, various goals, posts, volleyball standards and tunnels) – low tech, easy to make and deliver – at relatively high gross margins up to the 65% range. Proprietary product sales currently account for about $30 million of total revenue, a number which, while expected to be flat from '08 to '09, is expected to begin growing again as the economy recovers and institutional budgets expand, allowing for expanded purchasing of the larger, non-commodity expenditures the company's proprietary products represent, which are delayed in lean budget times. A higher mix of these higher margin products should help the company continue to boost overall gross margins, even while continuing its reduction in S,G&A expenses.

The company also derives revenues from strategic alliances. RBI maintains distribution rights for sports equipment from companies like Markers (field markers), Funnel (portable soccer equipment), Edwards, (tennis marketing/distribution), Equipment, Inc. (tennis accessory equipments), Mark One (camping equipment), and Diamond (baseball).

Given the company's dominant market position, any brand/ logo that wishes to enter the institutional sports market gets the greatest leverage by making a deal with RBI in order to tap into its turnkey distribution, which has lead to re-distribution of products under brands like Under ArmorTM, Rawlings and Wilson, which adds brand recognition to the company's product line-up and revenues. RBI is also the largest distributor of NikeTM team apparel (uniforms), and team apparel as a category represents about 42% ($100 million) of RBI's overall sales.

The company's speed to market and its ability to distribute/ deliver products quickly is one reason for the rapid expansion of revenues and institutional customers. RBI's offers the fastest shipping turnaround in the industry, 2-day delivery for all its manufactured products whereas the industry standard remains a sluggish 3-6 weeks!

This huge differentiator has allowed the company to attract new customers in large numbers. The company has experienced eleven straight years of revenue growth, with EBITDA accelerating faster than overall revenue -- a sign of tremendous operating leverage.

"COMPETITION" AS BUSINESS MODEL

The sporting goods and equipment industry, especially in the institutional markets is highly fragmented, and the absence of a barrier to entry leads to a bevy of small companies that, at best, merely survive, primarily due to lack of broad distribution and a largely regional focus. Historically, RBI's management has proven adept at identifying unique products that are selling well despite limited distribution, acquiring them at a multiple of current sales, then capturing a "distribution arbitrage" on the purchase by pumping the new products immediately through the company's vastly larger installed customer base and leveraging operating efficiencies and capital to make faster inventory turns (almost ten a year).

This management team has made over 100 acquisitions of companies in this highly fragmented space. The sports equipment industry is currently involved in a large-scale consolidation. Industry mainstays in the field such as Wilson and Spalding are primary involved in the retail space, still allowing for the leveraging of those brands to institutional customers, while companies like Riddell, MacGregor and Rawlings have at times advertised their availability for sale.

RBI potentially stands to benefit from the consolidation of some of these very companies into the RBI direct selling model, or even be acquired by a larger related company seeking a plug-and-play direct selling model.

STRONG OPERATING RESULTS, GROWTH IN A DOWN MARKET

Over the past several years, the overall institutional sporting goods industry has meandered across a $4 billion plateau, making few moves towards improvement and still highly fragmented. However, despite overall malaise in the industry and the downturn of the overall economy, RBI has remained an anomaly, growing every year since inception and recently taking advantage of operating leverage and efficiencies that have begun to generate substantial EBITDA - $12 million, $17 million and $24 million in FYs 2006, '07 and '08 respectively.

From FY 2006 to FY 2008, RBI increased its EBITDA by 100% on revenue growth of only 12% in the same period. Gross margins have continued to increase from 32% in FY 2006 to 36% in 2008, a level the company expects to maintain in FY 2009 despite the economic slowdown. Operating margins have more than doubled during the same period from 3.7% in 2006 to 7.8% in 2008. EPS doubled in each of those years, from $0.18 in 2006 to $0.38 and $0.76 in '07 and '08 respectively. While EPS has slowed down in the downturn, it is still forecast to be up 12% to $0.85 in FY '09, ending June 30. Commitment to, and migration of, substantial marketing, operational and transaction processes to the web should continue to reduce overhead. The company has no long-term debt and relatively significant borrowing power to use for opportunistic acquisitions.

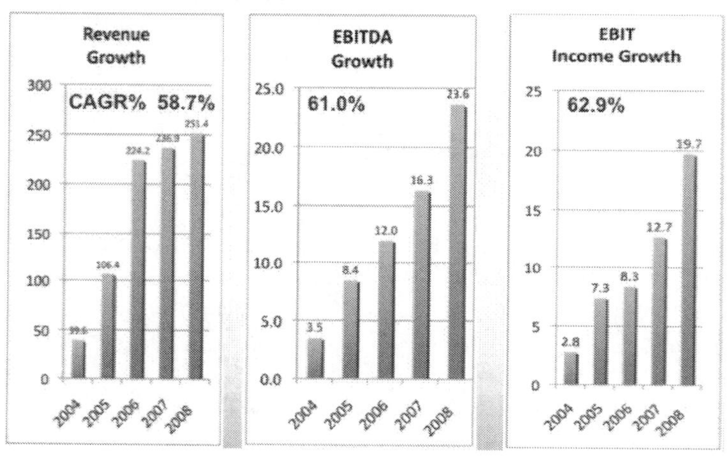

COMPARABLES, SORT OF

It is difficult to compare RBI apples-to-apples to any public competitor because it is the only publicly traded sports equipment manufacturer/distributor that sells exclusively to institutions.

In spite of this, RBI gets caught up inaccurately in the "retail sporting goods" net (because the company sees its primary competition as local sporting goods retailers) or even the "mail order catalogue" net (both consumer discretionary), and we believe the stock performance reflects this.

Case in point is that Big 5 Sporting Goods (BGFV) trades at double the P/E RBI does (18 vs. 9) despite the fact that BGFV has shown steady sales (-4%) and earnings (-50%) decline during the downturn while RBI has actually grown in both sales (+6%) and net income (+252%) during the same one-year period. While BGFV hit a 52-week high last week, RBI trades at barely 60% of its 52-week high.

Dick's Sporting Goods (DKS), the retail market leader, performed much closer to RBI with almost identical gross margin and income ratios (after accounting for extraordinary items – around 26% gross margin and 4% net income – and trades at 67% of its 52-week high. 17 analysts cover DKS and nine cover BGFV compared to only two for RBI. I think this creates my classic definition of "information arbitrage" and an opportunity for substantial price improvement.

RBI, which is showing considerably better relative operational performance than BGFV, better bottom line growth than DKS, would have to gain 100% ($15) just to be "in parity" with BGFV on a current P/E basis. DKS trades at a 13 P/E vs. 9 P/E for RBI, which leaves 44% to the upside in RBI ($13) just to trade in parity with DKS on this basis.

The true upside is even more when considering a forward P/E, as one must consider that, while retailers realize revenue growth primarily through the opening of new stores which creates substantial more overhead, RBI has reached a point of tremendous operating leverage, having added $7 million in operating income in the last fiscal year on just a sales increase of just $15 million because SG&A actually declined.

The stock trades at less than 40% of sales and right around book value compared to 2x book value and 50% of sales for DKS. To top it off and make this a "must buy," RBI pays a 1.4% dividend while you're waiting for the Street to catch up with the story.

A closer true comparable is School Specialty, Inc (SCHS), which markets supplemental educational materials – everyday consumables, instructional materials, educational games, art supplies, school forms, school furniture, and outdoor equipment – to schools and teachers – as well as product lines addressing the specific fields of arts, industrial arts, physical education, sciences, and early childhood, niche products to institutions, same as RBI.

SCHS sales and income were down 9% and 14% respectively in the latest quarter YoY, and yet the stock still carries a 12 P/E vs. RBI's 3% revenue slide but earnings growth trading at an 9 P/E. Once again, trading parity would suggest an $11 stock price, 50% up from the current price.

SHORT-TERM BUY WITH LONG TERM UPSIDE

RBI management has been a voracious acquirer of companies in the collective histories of the three companies they've run in this space, but have been out of the M&A market for the last two years, but in the current business climate valuations have dropped to attractive levels, and one can't help but think that the company will sooner than later begin to take advantage of its strong balance sheet (which includes potential liquidity in the form of an untapped $40 million credit facility, which is expandable to $60 million) to make some highly accretive deals. Investors have an opportunity to build positions in RBI during this "quiet time" and stand to benefit greatly from future company M&A activity. RBI now trades at $7.36 per share, barely 8x FY 2009 estimated EPS. Just eight months ago the stock was fairly liquid in the $11-12 range, and the fundamentals have gotten better.

RISKS

Low cash position, cash recently used to repay debt, improving

Budget cuts could affect customer buying, historically opposite effect

Limited liquidity, more liquidity seen at higher prices

COMPANIES MENTIONED

Dick's Sporting Goods (DKS)

Big 5 Sporting Goods (BGFV)

School Specialty, Inc. (SCHS)

CASE STUDY: TIX CORPORATION

KEY TAKEAWAYS:

Business model has counter-recessionary characteristics; discount-focused models drive unit volume growth even in a down market

Continued growth and operational improvement despite economic downturn; 260% average annual revenue growth from 2006 to 2008; accelerating cash flow

Significant operational leverage (increasing revenue $51mm in '08 while reducing overhead $3 million YoY) drives margin expansion – more on horizon

Debt-free

Recommendation: Buy rating with $4 price target; catalysts include quarterly reports showing increasing cash flow and the debut of the 101 Dalmatians show in September '09

BUSINESS DESCRIPTION

Tix Corporation is an integrated entertainment company providing "value family entertainment" ticketing services, event merchandising and the production and promotion of live entertainment. The company operates as three complimentary business units:

Tix4Tonight provides ticketing services including the operation of six kiosks in Las Vegas that provide last minute ticketing as well as providing premium ticketing services through its own web site (www.tix4anyevent.com) and private label ticketing for significant online retailers such as Costco Wholesale or the company's own web site (www.tix4members.com)

Exhibit Merchandising (EM) provides event/exhibit merchandise sales and services (The King Tut Store that tours with the exhibit)

Tix Productions Inc. (TPI), produces and promotes live entertainment shows.

THREE LEGS OF THE STOOL

Ticketing (20% of 2008 Revenue)

Six years ago TIXC brought the idea of selling discounted tickets to Las Vegas. When selling discounted tickets, Tix4Tonight generally sells them, from six different locations in Las Vegas, under short-term, exclusive and non-exclusive agreements with approximately 75 Las Vegas shows, offering tickets to more than 60 shows on any given day at a discount plus a service fee.

Tix4Tonight receives inventory for sale the same day on consignment directly from the show producer, artist or theater – a reflection of the Las Vegas market and its last minute purchasing pattern. Tix4Tonight does not know the exact number of tickets for each show it will be able to offer tickets for until the same day of the show.

The producers of the shows are paid on a weekly basis only for the tickets that Tix4Tonight actually sells to customers, so there is no financial risk with respect to unsold tickets and revenues are recorded at net of cost. Consequently ticket sales carry the highest gross margin of any business unit at 59%.

The growth opportunities in the Las Vegas operations are in growing event inventory by reaching agreements with additional shows, increasing the number of storefront locations and working to further monetize the relationships the company has with customers by offering complementary products and services such as offering discounted dining reservations tickets to approximately 30 Las Vegas area restaurants and discounted golf tee times to more than 30 Las Vegas golf courses.

The company recently announced the launch of an web-based platform, Tix4Members.com, to remove any constraints to growth that the limitation of physical locations might have created, and moves the company beyond the Las Vegas market.

Tix4Tonight also operates a national event ticket broker called Tix4AnyEvent.com, which offers premium tickets for sporting events, concert tours and theatres. Clients are usually national retail ticket brokers, with tickets sold being generally obtained through the event sponsor, artist or producer directly. Management is committed to expanding its event offerings through strong industry relationships.

Exhibit and Event Merchandising (16% of 2008 Revenue)

TIXC provides exhibit and event merchandising through its wholly-owned subsidiary, Exhibit Merchandising, LLC (EM). EM provides retail specialty stores for touring museum exhibitions and touring theatrical productions. EM provides a complete turn-key retail store including professional management and both custom-branded products and commercially-available products for sale.

EM operates the stores in space provided in conjunction with the exhibit. To date, revenues from the management of retail outlets associated with the sale of merchandise related to touring exhibits have been primarily derived from "Tutankhamen and The Golden Age of the Pharaohs." Management expects that EM's future growth will be from direct merchandising opportunities directed from other operating units, for example, Jesus Christ Superstar and Mannheim Steamroller, or by adding additional exhibits and events. EM, while operating at healthy gross margins in 2008 of 38%, produced operating losses in 2008 as a result of initiating operations and incurring higher cost of operations in Europe.

EM is expected to return to profitability in 2009 – and did so in Q1 '09) in light of the absence of European start-up costs, $33 million in goodwill and intangible asset impairment charges taken in December '08 and the reduction from $3 million in depreciation expenses reported in 2009.

Live Entertainment (64% of 2008 Revenue)

In January 2008, the Company created a new unit, Tix Productions, when it acquired and merged two live theatrical and concert production companies with long-standing reputations as leaders in their respective fields and a history of working together - Magic Arts & Entertainment, LLC (Magic) and NewSpace Entertainment, Inc. (NewSpace), the combination of which management believes will allow it to leverage resources, gain operating efficiencies and more fully utilize the combined network of producers and promoters.

This unit's model is to book touring theatrical and concert presentations with a history of successful commercial appeal (established brands/shows whose rights come up for renewal/bid or which are acquired by the company for the specific purpose of staging a production such as Dalmatians), thus limiting risk associated with de novo properties, as well as to participate in the development of new theatrical and concert presentations often originating on Broadway or London's West End.

In addition to traditional media, the company utilizes unique marketing assets to sell tickets, including its own substantial subscriber-based business (recurring revenue) in eight US cities and its Salt Lake City-based group sales team.

The company also occasionally invests in shows or productions in advance of their initial tour to obtain favorable touring and distribution rights, which are then sold to third-party presenters (who guarantee a certain level of ticket sales) and present opportunities for additional revenue (or cost-reduction) opportunities such as sponsorship (wherein a corporate sponsor underwrites a significant percentage of the production costs of a new show) – again greatly reducing risk.

Examples of this type of production are the tours of Mannheim Steamroller Christmas, Jesus Christ Superstar and the highly anticipated upcoming theatrical production of 101 Dalmatians® property. Shoring up the company's reputation as a leading provider of "value family entertainment" resistant to economic downturns, the average ticket price for a live event is $50.00 which is seen reasonable price and a value for most middle market consumers.

As presenters, Tix Productions generally contracts for entertainment properties from producers to present in specific company-selected multiple markets in the US and Canada, giving the company a distinct competitive advantage in that it allows the unit to work with shows throughout the country and negotiate terms that are unavailable to single presenters in individual markets.

For example, the company has substantial multi-show, subscriber-based programs, which greatly reduces risk associated with individual presentations, under the name "Broadway in (city name)" in eight U.S. cities, and in Canada under the name Canada Theatricals Live (now the second largest presenter of theaterbased events in Canada).

Opportunities for growth in the Live Entertainment unit revolve around expanding ownership of proprietary content, for example "Rain" – The Beatles Experience and Bob the Builder®, which gives the company first rights to present these shows and provides it with the ability to direct ticket sales and branded merchandising to other operating segments.

The strategies of "laying off" risk to third-party presenters (in the form of pre-sale guarantees) also limits profitability, and gross margins of 20% reflect this. Nonetheless, this business unit made a strong cash contribution in 2008 of $1.6 million on the backs of hits Lord of the Dance, Walking With Dinosaurs, and the previously mentioned shows, and is expected to grow substantially in 2009, especially if the staging of 101 Dalmatians® in September has the level of wide audience appeal that the company believes it will as well other productions throughout the year.

STRONG RESULTS, GROWTH IN A DECIMATED LAS VEGAS MARKET

"Even in the face of a down economy, entertainment remains a popular spending category," said Russ Crupnick, entertainment industry analyst for The NPD Group, April 17, 2009.

Not in Las Vegas over the past year. Various sources have estimated airline capacity cuts to Las Vegas at a mid-teens rate through the end of 2008. According to figures from the Las Vegas Convention and Visitors Authority: convention attendance declined 3.4%, and the economic impact of conventions fell 7.3%, with total convention room nights occupied dropping 12.7% for that period. Anecdotally for Q1 '09, MGM Mirage and Las Vegas Sands' Las Vegas operating properties saw YoY declines in revenue of 19% and 10% respectively in the quarter.

In the face of an unprecedented slowdown in Las Vegas, TIXC's Tix4Tonight discounted ticket service sold 44% more tickets to shows in Q1 '09 (ended March 31) than in same quarter in '08, generating a 66% increase in ticket revenue to $17.6 million.

Additionally, the Tix4Dinner business saw a 65% increase in dinner reservation revenue over prior year's comparable quarter. In Q1 '09, the company also made significant reductions in G&A, including an estimated $360,000/year in savings on royalty expenses in its merchandise store division. In February '09, the company launched its Tix4Members website in conjunction with an agreement with Costco, whose customers' "value" and "discount" mentality matches up with the company's offerings, and which, while expected to be a major growth driver for the company going forward as it seeks to add more "big box" customers, did not contribute materially to operational results in the quarter.

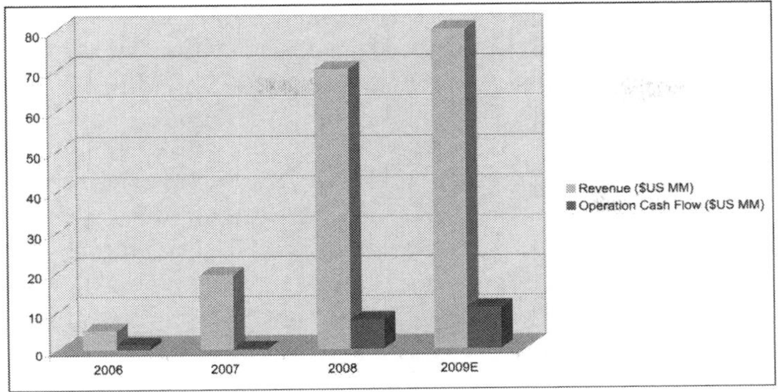

On a broader basis, the company continues to experience "hockey-stick" growth, growing revenue from $5 million to $19 million to $70 million in FY '06, '07 and '08 respectively, an average of 260% top line growth per year, while maintaining gross margins above 30%. The company even reduced G&A by $3 million in '07 from '08 despite a $51 million increase in revenue, demonstrating significant operational leverage in the model, and which allowed the company to generate $7.6 million in free cash – $0.21/share – in FY '08, a pace that picked up in Q1 '09 just reported.

With management expectations of 20-25% growth in ticket services and live entertainment (primarily on the strength of the highly anticipated 101 Dalmatians show), and a return to profitability of the merchandising unit, cash from operations in FY 2009 should top $10mm or $0.30 per share (Pre-GAAP) - $1.9 in cash flow in Q1 already - most dropping to net income since the company has an NOL offset.

COMPARABLES, COMPETITORS

Publicly-traded competitors in the ticketing space are Hollywood Media Corp (HOLL) and Ticketmaster Entertainment, Inc. (TKTM), neither of which offers the same-day discounted tickets service which is a huge growth engine for TIXC, although HOLL does offer Broadway dinner/theater packages. Yet, compare HOLL to TIXC and you'll see considerably different operating results in the same economic environment: HOLL saw a 5% decline in revenue from '07 to '08, suffering substantial negative cash flow and an erosion of tangible equity of $12 million, about half the equity on the balance sheet in the prior quarter.

TKMT has been able to grow revenue organically and through acquisitions (highly fragmented space), operating results which garnered a buyout/merger agreement with LiveNation (LYV) in a merger of debt-ridden, deteriorating net worth equals – this looks like a coup for LYV, as TKTM has the growth and cash flow, which will now be used to service LYV's debt.

Provided the merger passes anti-trust review, the combined companies currently trade at 7.5x TTM cash flow in consideration of 4% top line growth compared to TIXC, which trades at 7.5x TTM cash flow (and a near 300% top line growth rate and expanding cash flow), a discount to TKTM/LYV by a wide margin.

In the touring exhibits/shows space a reasonable competitor is Premier Exhibitions, Inc. (PRXI), which has had revenue declines amid tremendous operating, shareholder and legal issues but within the last 18 months traded at a 40x P/E based on hockey-stick growth in this space; in the exhibit store retail space, there are no direct public competitor and no other significant player.

Comparing the companies on the basis of multiple of operating cash flow, we find HOLL at N/A (negative cash flow), TKTM/LYV at 7.5x, PRXI at 15x and TIXC at 7.5x. All four trade at EV's at a fraction of revenue (from struggling HOLL, TKTM/LYV and PRXI at .25, 0.30 and 0.31 respectively to and TIXC at 0.64).

However, whereas combined TKTM/LYV has averaged about 9% annual revenue growth from FY '06 to FY '08, HOLL barely 5% (flat in most recent year) and PRXI revenue decline in FY '09 (ended February) of 14%, I believe TIXC's 260% annual revenue growth, as well as its having reached a current operating inflection point in which the company has begun to throw off significant cash, warrants a much higher multiple and price relative to the comps, placing a justifiable premium on future growth prospects. Simply stated, TIXC is and should continue to be a much faster grower than other players in its space, and its focus on "value entertainment" and discounts is making it more resilient in a downturn.

LONG TERM BUY

Not one analyst covers TIXC shares, making this the first report of its kind on the company, which I believe signals an opportunity to build a significant position in what is still a relatively quiet stock, but one I don't think will stay quiet, especially once it breaks through the $100 million market cap level and garner greater institutional reception.

TIXC trades at just 0.78x revenue, 68% off its 52-week high and barely above its low, this in spite of significant operating improvements through the year, during which time the company repurchased about $2.5 million worth of its shares at an average price of $2.57, 91% higher than where the shares trade today. Just eight months ago the stock was fairly liquid in the $4.00 range, and the fundamentals have gotten better.

The balance sheet is solid with virtually no debt and its largest-ever cash position at over $10 million, a virtual war chest in a buyers' market in the highly fragmented world of small entertainment properties and companies.

Even so, at just a 1520% projected growth in top line revenue and 50% growth in cash flow to $0.30/share for FY '09, a 15x multiple of cash flow is warranted in our opinion, reasonably valuing the stock on a mid-term (3-4 quarters) forward basis in the $4.00+ range, with "blue sky" upside depending on potentially high-impact results from new productions such as 101 Dalmatians®. On that basis TIXC is trading at 7.5x trailing FY 08 cash flow and only 5.3x FY 09 estimates.

RISKS

Historical losses, but now cash flow positive

Family and travel budget cuts could affect customer purchases, has been opposite so far

COMPANIES MENTIONED

Hollywood Media Corp. (HOLL)

Ticketmaster Entertainment, Inc. (TKMT)

Live Nation, Inc. (LYV)

Premier Exhibitions, Inc. (PRXI)

EPILOGUE:

TIXC is a classic example of how you can get just everything right and do just everything right with a microcap and still pay a price for things not entirely related to the business. TIXC was (and is) a great little company with exciting and diverse lines of business in the entertainment space. The stock tripled in the months following my recommendation (and I'm sure lots of my readers at the time cashed out), but I liked it a lot for the long term and stayed with it. Unfortunately, an internal management decision was made to voluntarily de-list the stock from the OTC Bulletin Board to the Pink Sheets, which meant the company would no longer report audited results. Many investors don't like this. I didn't like it. The stock suffered, plunging for a while to below my recommend price.

However, here we are five years later and the company is reporting again and the stock is about 50% higher than where I recommended it, making this "loser" actually a 9% a year producer, plus the stock pays a 9% dividend. The story has changed and isn't as attractive to me as it once was, but it's still been a "plus" pick because the fundamentals continued to be solid even as the stock dropped because of non-company related reasons, but rather "mechanical" reasons - the delisting. This is why we diversify! You can't see around every corner.

CASE STUDY: TVI CORPORATION

Technological advancements typically fall into two separate camps. On the one hand are those innovations and inventions that we never knew we were missing until they were released, such as the internet and the cell phone. On the other hand there are those products and services that fill a demand gap -- products that BECOME needed. Often times, these products already exist, but a certain event, or social change brings about their proliferation.

Just as there is no certain way to foresee future geo-social and geopolitical affairs or catastrophes, there is no way to predict which of the latter camp will be in demand. However, by honing in on the in-demand company and product line at the right time, one can effectively capitalize on a company's future demand and earnings growth.

In this issue of Bull Market MicroCap Review, we profile one such company, TVI (TVIN, $1.23). TVI is a Maryland-based company, whose principal activity is to design, manufacture and market rapidly deployable, integrated shelter systems. TVI has become the premier supplier and developer of temporary structures that need to be "raise-able" in minutes (i.e., an 11x21x8-ft high structure in 10 minutes by four people) in time-sensitive, crisis scenarios. Such structures developed by TVI include decontamination units -- the types deployed at suspected chemical weapons/hazmat sites. By virtue of their product line and understanding of the needs of the market, the company has filled a demand gap -- one exacerbated by the September 11th 2001 terrorist attacks and America's ongoing war on terrorism. TVI is the only large-scale provider of these services, and has garnered contracts across the United States and around the world.

Being in the right place at the right time with the right product has allowed TVI to see growth in revenues from just $3 million a few years ago to a projected $20 million+ this year.

PRODUCT LINE

Before we delve into our analysis of the company, it is fundamental to understand what exactly TVI does. Under the umbrella of decontamination units, TVI manufactures convenient and rapidly constructible shelter systems to protect soldiers, workers, victims and patients from chemical, biological, hazardous material and other dangers. The company also manufactures integrated systems for decontamination, command control, forensic investigation, disaster assistance, communication centers and patient isolation. These systems are geared for institutional use, and have been popularized by the military, public health, and first response agencies.

TVI's articulating frame (the rapidly deployed frame that forms the shelters) has a series of patents, and can be installed by just one person in a matter of minutes. In addition to shelters, TVI supplies lighting, water heaters, air heaters, power generators, flooring, trailers and air filtration units. Moreover, the group has a thermal products division, which manufactures thermal signature targets for live fire gunnery, and camouflage, concealment and deception devices.

TVI's forte, however remains its decontamination units. They are light, convenient, and come in many varieties depending on the medical, military or institutional needs of the customer. It is quite a sight to tour the company's manufacturing facilities, which we have done, and see a virtual football field under one roof crammed wall-to-wall with these shelters, which are all being built to specification, and all going out the back door to be delivered as fast as they can be built.

In total, the company earns 90% of its revenues from the shelter and decontamination shelter product line and 10% from thermal targets.

GEOPOLITICAL EVENTS

The first bullet point highlighting our endorsement of TVI comes by virtue of a shift in the global geopolitical landscape. Since the September 11th terrorist attacks, the rules of global warfare have changed. The free world's greatest enemy no longer fights front line battles in the trenches. Nor does the enemy attempt to match the firepower and technology of the United States and its allies. Such a strategy proved useless during the first Gulf War, and now the new terrorist enemy has adapted to strike where America is weakest.

As 9/11 illustrated, terrorists have shown no bounds in their evil, and will seek ways to destroy American and international interests in the most covert, damaging ways, through the use of unconventional weapons. This new breed of warfare makes America's large and immobile military inapplicable in many situations. Moreover, the threat on America's home turf exposed a logistical vulnerability in dealing with a potential large-scale biochemical attack.

On the offensive, as America shifts its reliance in the War on Terror to a rapidly deployable, tactile, small scale military unit, it will need equally mobile decontamination and other shelters, such as the ones provided by TVI. On the defensive, as the world battens down the hatches in preparation for another terrorist attack, there is needed a rapidly deployable, hazmat/decontamination unit. With these two major factors in scope, the stage has been set for TVI's rapid growth of the last few years and going forward.

Among the first on the scene following the 9/11 terrorist attack at the Pentagon, TVI erected decontamination units within moments, providing aid workers with immediate and sturdy shelters to care for America's terrorist victims. The decontamination units were essentially what the doctor ordered in America's greatest time of need, and were noticed by public officials and private enterprises as an immediate solution for the unthinkable.

RECENT CONTRACTS SIGNED

America and the free world needs to prepare for the unthinkable. Therefore, building upon its already strong reputation as a patriot company capable of delivering essential equipment in the darkest hours, TVI has been busy signing contracts with the National Government, Homeland Security, and a plethora of state hospitals. In addition, the company has attracted global celebrity. In May, TVI signed a major contract with the United Kingdom's government regarding Operation Iraqi Freedom, and has formed a strategic alliance with UK-based Professional Protection Systems, the makers of the Plysu decontamination systems used in the aftermath of the 1995 sarin gas subway attack in Tokyo.

Notable TVI Corporate Contracts

Customer	Size	Date
Wash. State 1st Responders/Hospitals	$2.2 M	Jun '03
Brit Fire Svc Decontamination	$285,000	Sep '03
California State Hospitals	$1.7 M	Sep '03
Department of Veteran Affairs	$2 M	July '03
UK Operation Iraqi Freedom	$8.9 M	May '03
Office for Homeland Security	$385,000	Mar '03
Mass Emergency Mgmt Agency	$3 M	Dec '02

As threats of bio-chemical attacks in our cities loom, there inevitably (and unfortunately) will be a need for rapidly deployable decontamination and hazmat units.

Furthermore, as America attempts to carve out the terrorist infrastructure on foreign soil, so too will it need to prepare for the enemy's use of unconventional and biochemical weapons. With America fundamentally restructuring both its offensive strategy and its defensive capabilities in combating the effects of terrorism, TVI stands to grow rapidly into the foreseeable future.

FINANCIAL PERFORMANCE

By virtue of the current climate, and the surge in demand for its products, TVI's financial position is growing. In addition to the expansion of the company's customer base, TVI reported income growth of just $100,000 in 2001 to over $3 million in 2002 on a 150%+ increase in revenues. What we find the most powerful and impressive, is the sustainability and consistency of the growth.

KEY FINANCIAL DATA	
Ticker Symbol:	TVIN
52-Week High:	$1.77
52-Week Low:	$0.43
Market Cap:	$33 million
PE:	7
PEG:	0.08
Price/Book:	3.8
Shares Outstanding:	29 million

For example, in 2Q03, TVI reported net income of $1.2 million on $6.8 million in revenue, a year-over year increase of 300%. Basic earnings per share in the second quarter increased 275% to $0.04 from $0.01 in the same period a year ago. When considered on a half-year basis, we see sales of $12.4 million, representing a 260% increase over the first six months of 2002.

Net income for the six months ended June 30th increased 360% over the first six months of 2002 to $2.4 million. EPS increased 330% to $0.08 from just 2 cents in the same six-month period last year. When surveying the trailing 12 months, EPS was 22 cents. In total, by the end of the second quarter, TVI had a backlog of nearly $6.2 million, representing the likely continuation of sound revenue growth and cash flow.

The financial position is strong. Book value increased from $2.3 million to $8.7 million in the past year. Buffered by $3.3 million in cash and growing (an increase of 500% over June 2002), the company has the reserve, order backlog, reputation, and strategic alliances to ensure strong growth. Add to the fact that TVI in August achieved recognition in The Washington Post as having the third largest revenue growth of any firm in the region for 2002. The Daily Record (Maryland) gave them the "Top Innovator of the Year 2003" designation. The company is finally getting some recognition for its product line and business success. As we have noted in the past, improved positive publicity and coverage will likely be beneficial to a company's shares.

FINANCIAL ANALYSIS

TVI's financial position shows strong growth, though the company remains undervalued. Because the company has languished on the OTC Bulletin Board, TVI falls below the radar screen of most investors. At $1.23 a share, the company's shares maintain a PE ratio of 7 -- a low number for a company that is likely to grow by 50-100%.

However, when we examine our favorite trading metric, the company's PEG ratio, the generally low number becomes dramatically lower. From 2001 through 2002, the company's sales -- with earnings keeping pace -- grew 200%. Based upon the large contracts already signed, TVI's 2003 sales will grow to be over $20 million, a 100% increase over 2002, with a similar 50% increase in earnings expected. Therefore, since the stock is trading at just 7x earnings, TVI's PEG is an astoundingly low 0.14.

We strongly believe that TVI's shares are dramatically undervalued, and we project that with the increased contracts, publicity and coverage, they will appreciate considerably. We think the firm will do $6 million in profits this year, double last year. Management has confirmed this. This is amazing for a firm worth only $33 million.

Our standard for a well-priced stock as related to its growth rate is a PEG of 1.0, a company with a PE of exactly its growth rate. We'd like to think that TVI's shares can increase enough to provide a PE of 20, which is a PEG of just 0.20, at the 100% growth rate that we foresee for 2003 and 2004, giving us a realistic target of $5-6 a share within the next year. This would be a 4- to 5-bagger. Even if it takes two years, we'd be quite pleased.

We expect earnings to continue to increase consistently over the next few years. Regardless of the country's executive leadership, America appears committed to the War on Terror, and small-scale, precision military attacks supported by TVI decontamination and other specialized shelters will likely continue to be the prevailing military trend.

MANAGEMENT

Finally, we like TVI's management team, some members of which we've had a many-years relationship with. Led by CEO Rick Priddy, the company has the managerial expertise and professional relationships to continue to thrive. On the one hand, TVI's executives and directors are the pioneers in this niche market and understand how to manufacture, develop and market rapidly deployable decontamination units. On the other hand, management has the necessary relationships and diplomatic ties to ensure that the company stays on top of current trends in the military. One example is new director Harley Hughes, who is a former Lieutenant General for the U.S. Air Force, and served both as Deputy Chief of Staff for Plans and Operations, and the Air Force Operations Deputy to the Joint Chief of Staff. In essence, management maintains an effective mix of technical expertise and relationship savvy -- a combination that will continue to help forge business building strategic alliances and contracts.

CONCLUSION

Our endorsement of TVI is rooted both in qualitative and quantitative reasons. TVI fills an important demand gap left gaping open following America's waged global war on terror. As the world becomes increasingly vigilant to prepare to mitigate the effects of another surprise attack, products such as those manufactured and deployed by TVI will be in increasing demand.

The shares of TVI remain significantly undervalued, and we believe that it won't be long before the large contracts and awards given get noticed by the broader marketplace, sending the stock to more appropriate levels. It's just not too often that you get the chance to buy shares in a company trading at less than 15% of its three-year growth rate. To reiterate, we believe there is upside in the stock to at least $6 by the end of 2004.

EPILOGUE:

TVIN is easily the worst overall situation among my picks. When I looked at it, it had everything going for it, blistering growth, proprietary products, strong customers. And the stock performed accordingly for a while after my recommendation, rising more than 300% in less than a year (from $1.23 to $6.00). I made my sell recommendation at about half that, locking in a 177% return.

Subsequently, management turns out to have been skimming money and engaging in all types of impropriety, which ultimately led to the company's implosion and the stock going to $0.

Lots of people made money along the way, but it's another cautionary tale highlighting the need to diversify and remain disciplined and unemotional when it comes time to move out of a position when price gets to where it represents fair value relative to the underlying fundamentals.

Made in the USA
Columbia, SC
05 May 2017